WITHDRAWN

Kuwait

Kuwait

BY TERRI WILLIS

Enchantment of the World
Second Series

Children's Press®

A Division of Scholastic Inc.

NEW YORK   TORONTO   LONDON   AUCKLAND   SYDNEY
MEXICO CITY   NEW DELHI   HONG KONG
DANBURY, CONNECTICUT

Frontispiece: Camels in the Kuwaiti desert

Consultant: Peter Sluglett, Professor of Middle Eastern History, University of Utah, Salt Lake City

Please note: *All statistics are as up-to-date as possible at the time of publication.*

Book production by Herman Adler

Library of Congress Cataloging-in-Publication Data

Willis, Terri.
  Kuwait / by Terri Willis.
    p. cm. — (Enchantment of the world. Second series)
  ISBN-13: 978-0-516-24902-5
  ISBN-10: 0-516-24902-9
  1. Kuwait—Juvenile literature. I. Title. II. Series.
  DS247.K8W55 2007
  953.67—dc22   2006010385

© 2007 by Terri Willis.
All rights reserved. Published in 2007 by Children's Press, an imprint of Scholastic Library Publishing. Published simultaneously in Canada.
Printed in the United States of America.

CHILDREN'S PRESS and associated logos are trademarks and/or registered trademarks of Scholastic Library Publishing. SCHOLASTIC and associated logos are trademarks and/or registered trademarks of Scholastic Inc.
1 2 3 4 5 6 7 8 9 10 R 16 15 14 13 12 11 10 09 08 07

Kuwait

Contents

Cover photo:
Safat Square

Kuwait City

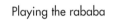
Playing the rababa

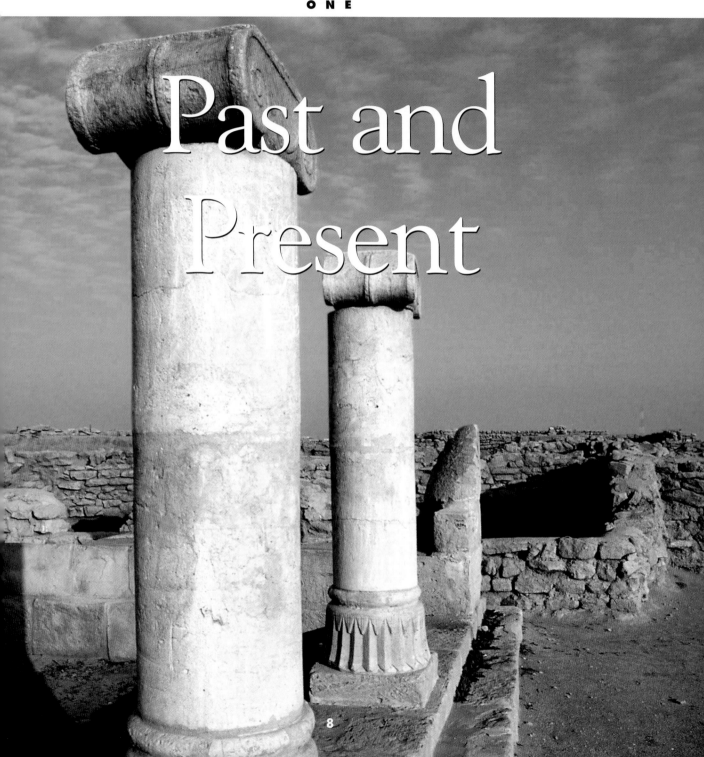

Past and Present

8

Kuwaitis have a particular talent for keeping pieces of their past alive. Their country has had its share of turning points, moments in history when something happens and nothing is quite the same again. But in Kuwait, the past is never completely abandoned.

Kuwait was a poor country that quickly became wealthy. It went from being a completely independent nation to being invaded and occupied by a hostile country in a matter of hours. And then, after several terrible months, it was free again.

Opposite: **Greek ruins on the Kuwaiti island of Faylaka date back more than two thousand years.**

Many modern towers rise in Kuwait City.

In Kuwait's early days, families were the basic unit of society. People lived, worked, and socialized within their large, extended family groups—their tribes. Today, in a nation filled with cell phones and fast cars, airplanes and computers, it would be easy to move beyond those family bonds. But in Kuwait, the family is as strong and important as ever.

In this same country, with all its modern equipment and high-tech gadgets, one of the most beloved sports remains camel racing. This sport has been popular in Kuwait for centuries. But today, the camels aren't ridden by young boys, as they were in the past. There were too many complaints that the sport was dangerous and that the children were mistreated. Now the camels have small robots riding them, robots that are dressed to look like young boys. The past and present constantly mingle in Kuwait.

Kuwait began using robot jockeys in 2006. The robots are operated by remote control.

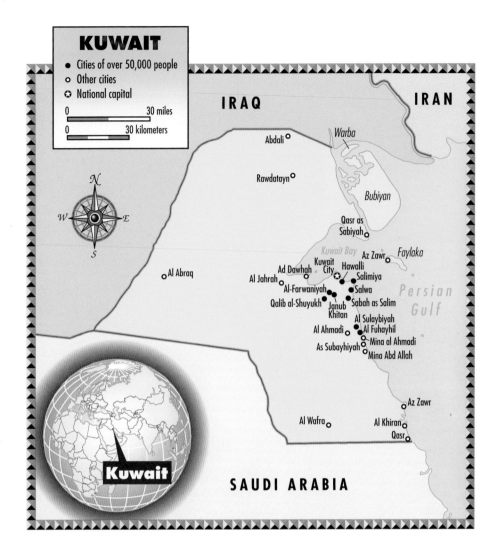

Kuwait sits upon vast reserves of oil. This oil has made the nation incredibly wealthy. It has also made Kuwait a target for other nations eager to grab hold of its riches.

In 1990, Kuwait's neighbor Iraq, led by Saddam Hussein, invaded Kuwait. This was the start of the Gulf War. The war only lasted a few months, but in that time, Iraqi troops caused massive destruction in Kuwait. People were tortured and

The Iraqi invasion devastated Kuwait. Many buildings were wrecked or burned.

killed. Buildings and roads were demolished. The environment was seriously damaged. It was hard to return to normal life.

The Diwaniya

The diwaniya has been a Kuwaiti custom for generations. Diwaniyas are male gatherings, usually held in the evening in special rooms or tents. The men often gather several times a week. They sit in comfortable chairs and snack on food supplied by their host.

The focus of diwaniyas is conversation. The men discuss a wide variety of topics—local and international politics, social problems, the economy. Some people feel that diwaniyas are evidence that people in Kuwait have more freedom than people in some other Middle Eastern countries. The diwaniya shows that Kuwaitis can freely discuss issues without fear.

But the Kuwaitis found a way. They went back to prayer and to school and to work. They again found strength in their families and in their traditions. Political discussion once again thrived in meetings called *diwaniyas*. Life returned to normal.

Because of the wealth and modernization that are common in Kuwait, a snapshot of life in Kuwait would look much like life in Western nations. Most Kuwaitis have plenty of costly possessions—nice cars, cell phones, digital cameras, computers, all the latest technology. They like the latest music, and their homes have all the modern comforts.

But that snapshot wouldn't show how Kuwaitis live with all these possessions, and that is what sets them apart from people in the West. Their time revolves around family, the most important social group in the lives of most Arabs. Large gatherings with extended family are common. Their Muslim faith affects all aspects of life. They pray five times a day. Their faith influences the clothes they wear and the food they eat. Throughout their daily lives, Kuwaitis blend the modern and the traditional in a mix that serves them well.

A Desert Land

Kuwait's Burgan oil field is the second-largest oil field in the world. Only Ghawar, in Saudi Arabia, is larger.

KUWAIT IS MOSTLY FLAT AND MOSTLY DESERT. LESS than 1 percent of the country can be used as farmland to grow food, and there is limited freshwater underground for drinking. But the area that is now Kuwait has been home to people for thousands of years. Today, Kuwait, which is slightly smaller than the state of New Jersey, supports more than two million people.

Why do so many people live in a barren desert? At least part of the answer lies under the ground—in vast, murky, black pools. Kuwait has massive stores of oil, more than nearly any other country. That oil creates jobs and wealth for its people. It is what keeps most people living in this tiny nation.

Opposite: **Most of Kuwait is dry and waterless.**

Kuwait produces 2.5 million barrels of oil every day.

A Middle Eastern Nation

Kuwait is in the Middle East, the part of the world where Asia and Africa meet. There is some disagreement about which countries actually make up the Middle East. Those countries most often identified as Middle Eastern are Kuwait, Bahrain, Cyprus, Egypt, Iran, Iraq, Israel, Jordan, Qatar, Lebanon, Oman, Saudi Arabia, Syria, Turkey, the United Arab Emirates, and the Yemen Arab Republic.

Though most Middle Eastern land is desert, it's not wasteland. Much of it sits atop valuable oil fields. The Middle East produces most of the world's oil, more than twenty million barrels each day. Kuwait's oil reserve ranks fourth among Middle Eastern countries. The much larger nations of Saudi Arabia, Iraq, and Iran rank ahead of it.

Too Salty to Drink

Kuwait is a very dry country, so finding fresh drinking water has always been difficult. In many parts of the world, water from under the ground can be pumped up and used as drinking water. But Kuwait has little groundwater. The nation has a long coastline on the Persian Gulf, but its water is too salty to drink.

To make salt water drinkable, the salt must be removed. This process is called desalination. It usually involves heating the water to boiling. The water forms steam that evaporates, leaving the salt behind. The steam is captured and condensed into drinking water.

Desalination is costly because of the energy needed to heat the water and then cool the steam. Nearly all Kuwait's freshwater—95 percent—comes from desalination plants.

The Lay of the Land

What does the Kuwaiti landscape look like? The tiny country is wedged in between the much larger nations of Saudi Arabia and Iraq at the northwestern tip of the Persian Gulf. Iran is not far away.

Kuwait is mainly flat, pebbly desert, ground down from rock created some twenty-five million years ago. Over millions of years, wind, waves, sandstorms, and rain wore down the rock, forming the sand and gravel. These same conditions helped shape Kuwait's landscape, making some low, rolling hills. Most of Kuwait is less than 660 feet (200 meters) above sea level. The country has no mountains or rivers and few natural features.

Camels and sheep graze on Kuwait's meager grasses.

In the desert are a few *wadis*, dry river beds that fill with water during the occasional heavy rains. Shallow depressions in the desert also fill after the rains, providing water for desert dwellers and camel herds.

The tallest point in the country is an unnamed spot that rises to just over 1,000 feet (300 m). Another high point

Al-Mutla Ridge is one of the highest points in Kuwait. It lies in the northern part of the country about 5 miles (8 km) from the Iraqi border.

Kuwait's Geographic Features

Area: 6,880 square miles (17,818 km)

Greatest Distance North to South: 115 miles (185 km)

Greatest Distance East to West: 129 miles (208 km)

Land and Water Borders: Saudi Arabia to the south, Iraq to the north and west, and the Persian Gulf to the east.

Inland Bodies of Water: Kuwait has no major rivers or lakes

Lowest Elevation: Sea level, along the coastline

Highest Elevation: An unnamed hill, 1,004 feet (306 m) above sea level

Average Daily Temperature: 91°F (33°C)

Average Annual Precipitation: 4 inches (10 cm)

became well known in the Gulf War. A major massacre occurred at al-Mutla Ridge when coalition aircraft fired on Iraqi forces retreating along it.

Kuwait's coastline, which runs for 180 miles (290 kilometers) along the Persian Gulf, has few remarkable features. Gently sloping sand dunes are common along the shore. Salt marshes are found in the bay near Kuwait City.

Mubarak the Great

Shaikh Mubarak al-Sabah, the leader of Kuwait from 1896 to 1915, is often called Mubarak the Great, *Mubarak al-Kabir* in Arabic. He took control of the country after murdering his brother, who had been its leader. Despite the bloody start to Mubarak's reign, he is loved by many Kuwaitis for all the good he did for their country. Mubarak reached out to the Bedouin, the region's nomadic desert people, who had battled the Kuwaiti government, and he won their support. He resisted pressure from foreign powers, such as the Ottoman Empire and Germany, that wanted to control or occupy parts of Kuwait. Under Mubarak's reign, the country's northern boundaries were settled, but Mubarak gave up no land.

Through his strong and effective leadership, Mubarak the Great raised the status of Kuwait throughout the world. He is also the namesake for the country's newest governorate, called Mubarak al-Kabir. Kuwait has six governorates, which are similar to states and provinces. Mubarak al-Kabir was formed in 2000, when the Hawalli governorate was split in two. It has about 177,000 residents.

Islands

Nine islands off of Kuwait's coast are part of the country. The largest are Bubiyan, Faylaka, and Warba. Though Bubiyan is the biggest, no one lives there. It is mostly marsh. Faylaka is the island with the most residents.

Qaruh is the smallest of Kuwait's nine islands. It was the first part of Kuwait to be freed from Iraqi occupation during the Gulf War.

People first lived on Faylaka Island some five thousand years ago. The island still holds clues about the lives of these people—it is the country's premier archaeological site. Faylaka Island lies about 12 miles (20 km) off the coast. It is linked to Kuwait City by several underwater power cables and pipelines that deliver drinking water. Faylaka is also one of the country's top tourist attractions. People go there to swim and sail in the beautiful waters.

Faylaka was once the site of a thriving Greek settlement. Archaeologists have uncovered the remains of homes, temples, and roads.

The Gulf Waters

In the east, Kuwait borders the Persian Gulf. Kuwait Bay takes a big bite out of the coastline at Kuwait City. The water off the northern coastline, especially along the bay, is shallow, less than 15 feet (5 m) deep, and the bottom is mostly muddy.

Most Kuwaitis live in cities along the Persian Gulf coast.

These conditions are not good for shipping. Most of Kuwait's shipping ports are along the southern Gulf coast. The water is deeper there, making it possible for large ships to maneuver.

Kuwait has six major seaports and some twenty more ports where smaller boats can dock. About one-quarter of the nation's shoreline is set aside for recreation. The remaining coast is divided roughly equally between land that businesses have built on and land that has been left in its natural state.

Damage from the War

The Gulf War caused massive destruction to the environment. Nearly one-third of Kuwait's land was damaged in some way. The war seriously disturbed the top layer of desert soil throughout much of the country. Land mines were planted, trenches were dug, and heavy military vehicles stormed over

Sunken Ships

Many ships sank in the waters off Kuwait during the conflicts of the recent years. These sunken ships are causing serious environmental problems.

Many went down with their cargo still aboard—cargo such as fertilizers, refined fuels, and ammunition. These pollutants slowly leak out of the sunken ships, and currents carry them far into the Persian Gulf. These chemicals can contaminate the desalination plants that provide Kuwaitis with their drinking water.

Sunken ships pose other dangers. Some contain bombs and mines that could explode and cause serious damage. In addition, underwater plants and animals are being harmed both by the pollution and by the huge obstructions in their habitats. Ships that sink in shallow water also can cut off ocean traffic at seaports, as has already happened in Iraq.

A recent survey pinpointed 282 sunken ships in the northern Persian Gulf, but there are probably hundreds more. A plan to remove the 40 largest shipwrecks began in 2004. The cost is high, as much as $8 million per ship, but the dangers posed by the ships make their removal necessary.

the land. Some sand was ground into smaller grains. Deeper, small-grained sand was also exposed. Kuwait's strong winds easily blew this small-grained sand about. It gathered in giant clouds and was dropped in new areas, changing the landscape. Several important military buildings nearly disappeared under the sand, roads were covered, and some of the nation's few farms were buried.

More than seven hundred oil wells were set on fire by Iraqi troops, doing even more damage. The smoke that blew across the land contained tiny oil droplets and soot that landed and mixed with the soil and sand. As this mixture dried and hardened, it formed a tarlike layer as much as 5 inches (12 centimeters) thick. The oil also pooled above the surface in about two hundred small "oil lakes." Dangerous chemicals contained in these lakes seeped downward, poisoning the groundwater.

Men protect their faces during a dust storm. The howling dust can sting the eyes and make breathing difficult.

Climate

Kuwait is a desert. It is often brutally hot, but not always. The temperature ranges between freezing and broiling, depending on the season and the time of day, but the overall average daily temperature is 91 degrees Fahrenheit (33 degrees Celsius). August is the hottest month, with an average high temperature of 112°F (44°C). In January, the average low temperature dips to 45°F (7°C). The highest temperature ever recorded in Kuwait was 126°F (52°C).

During the long, dry summers of May through October, temperatures are high, but the air is not as humid as in other Gulf states. Dust storms sometimes rage for several days during the summer, choking entire cities. Kuwait gets the bulk of its rainfall during the winter, usually between 1 and 7 inches (3 and 8 cm) each year.

Kuwait's weather was once quite different. Some five hundred thousand to two million years ago, it rained heavily in the region. The little groundwater that Kuwait has today came from these rains long ago. It filtered down through the soil and gathered in deep pools. Today, these pools of ancient water are tapped to supply a small amount of the country's freshwater.

A Look at Kuwait's Cities

Kuwait City (above), the capital, is located at the mouth of Kuwait Bay. The city itself is fairly small, with only about 32,600 residents. But several other larger cities lie in the metropolitan region surrounding the capital, and this is where most Kuwaitis live.

Qalib al-Shuyukh, with 179,264 residents, is the nation's largest city, followed by Salimiya, with 145,328 residents. The next three largest cities and their populations are Hawalli, 106,992; Janub Khitan, 92,646; and al-Farwaniyah, 83,544.

All of these cities are growing fast. Salimiya has a modern, beautiful pyramid-shaped mosque (right). Hawalli is home to the Tariq Rajab Museum and its unique collection of Islamic art. Many of Hawalli's old buildings are being torn down to make room for shopping centers and apartment buildings.

Surviving the Desert

THE PLANTS AND ANIMALS THAT LIVE IN KUWAIT MUST BE able to survive in a harsh environment. Scorching temperatures and little rainfall challenge them to find ways to grow.

The air temperature in Kuwait commonly reaches more than 100°F (40°C). The temperature on the ground can reach nearly 180°F (80°C). That's not much cooler than the temperature at which water starts to boil! To survive in such an environment, plants and animals must adapt to heat and lack of water.

Opposite: **Kuwait's camels are dromedary camels, which have only one hump.**

Many plants in Kuwait have thick leaves in which they store moisture.

Wildflowers burst quickly into bloom after rains, bringing rare color to the desert.

Plants in the Desert

Bushy clumps of grasses are common in the desert that covers most of Kuwait. In low areas of the desert where water can gather, flowers bloom after the rains. These plants survive heat and drought by forming seeds that lie dormant, sometimes for years. When the water arrives, they quickly burst into bloom. For these brief periods, the desert is alive with color. The vivid display doesn't last long—the blooming plants usually survive only a few days.

The National Flower

Kuwait's national flower is the *arfaj,* a desert shrub that can grow to more than 2 feet (60 cm) tall. Each spring, the shrub fills with sweet-smelling golden yellow flowers. Bedouin sometimes use this plant as firewood.

Kuwait's Only Trees

The only trees native to Kuwait are date palms, which grow in desert oases. People have also planted date palms in yards and parks and along streets, so they are common in Kuwait. Date palms grow to 60 feet (18 m) tall, with fronds up to 9 feet (3 m) long. Branching spikes on the trees produce the dates. Each spike can carry as many as a thousand dates, and a single tree produces about 600 pounds (270 kilograms) of fruit in a season. Dates are unusually sweet, about 70 percent sugar. The high sugar content helps the dates survive longer in the extreme heat, so they don't rot as quickly as other tropical fruits would.

Bedouin once depended on date palms for their survival in the desert. The dates were an important food source, of course, but the Bedouin also used the tree to make all kinds of useful items. Often, the trunks became columns and beams for houses, and the fronds were used for walls and ceilings. The fronds were also woven into sandals, baskets, and mats. No part of the date palm was wasted.

Grassy plants grow in the sand dunes near the coast. Their roots help hold the soil in place during heavy winds. Small shrubs also grow in the sand dunes. Plants living on the dunes and in the desert have long roots that can tap into the groundwater deep below. Desert plants usually grow some distance from one another, so they can each get enough water. Often, their leaves are small and waxy. This prevents the water in the leaves from evaporating. Many desert shrubs can absorb some water from the air as well. During the cooler, wetter times of

The desert horned viper burrows into the sand to escape the heat of the day. It emerges at night to hunt small animals and birds.

year, the plants store nutrients in their roots to help them survive when the weather turns hot and dry. Plants that can do this are called succulents.

Animals Adapt

Animal life in Kuwait's desert is closely tied to plant life. Plants provide food for the animals, and some offer cooling shade during the day. Just as plants must adapt to the harsh desert conditions, so must animals.

Desert animals usually have light coloring. This helps them blend in with the background of sand and rocks so that their enemies have difficulty finding them. The light coloring also reflects light and heat, keeping the animals from overheating. Some small creatures stay cool by burrowing under the sand. They often have special coverings over the eyes, ears, and nose to help keep out grains of sand.

Of all the animals that have adapted to life in the desert, the most famous is probably the camel. Kuwait's camels have just one hump.

Camels

Camels played a large role in Kuwaiti history. The country's early Bedouin depended on camels to travel through the desert. The camels carried the people and their goods—up to 1,000 pounds (450 kilograms)—across the hot, loose sand. This earned them the nickname "ships of the desert." Camels also provided people with meat and milk. Without this ready supply of camel milk, the Bedouin would have needed far more water than was usually available in the desert.

Bedouin have long relied on camels to survive in the desert. Camel milk is more nutritious than cow milk, with higher levels of iron and vitamin C.

Camels helped in other ways, too. Bedouin gathered and wove the soft hair from camel bellies to make their tents. Dried camel skin was made into leather bags, and dried camel manure was good fuel for burning in a fire.

A camel can live for weeks without water, and can smell water up to 1 mile (1.6 km) away. When it finally reaches water, it makes the most of it. It can drink 25 gallons (95 liters) at one time! A camel can also store about 50 gallons (200 liters) of water in three different sections of its stomach. The camel uses its hump, which is a large lump of fat, for nourishment when no other food or water is available. As this fat is used, the hump gets smaller and slumps to one side.

Camels have other features that allow them to thrive in the desert. They can live on the pits of dates and the leaves and stems of thorny desert shrubs. They can close their eyes and

Horses of the Desert

Kuwait's Bedouin once used horses for transportation. The Bedouin had great respect and affection for their horses, and rarely sold or lent them to others. Purebred Arabian horses were especially prized. The Bedouin took great care to trace their horses' ancestries, just as they traced their own.

Today, equestrian sports—those that involve horses—are popular in Kuwait. The national show-jumping team has won many medals in international competitions. Kuwait also has a hunting and equestrian club. All of the club's horses were stolen during the Iraqi invasion, but they were replaced within two years.

nostrils so tightly during a dust storm that not one speck of sand gets in. The leathery soles of their feet are big and wide, just right for walking across the sand without sinking in.

Other Desert Animals

Camels are by far the most visible animals in Kuwait. Other desert animals stay mostly tucked out of sight. Desert mammals usually sleep during the heat of the day and move about at night when it is cooler.

Small mammals that thrive in the Kuwaiti desert include jerboas, desert hares, and sand rats, which are basically the same as gerbils. Sand rats don't need much water. At night, they hunt for insects, grasses, and seeds. Jerboas look something like tiny kangaroos. They have short front legs and long hind legs that they use for jumping. They can leap up to 8 feet (2.5 m) in one bound. Their long tails help balance them for their jumps.

The fennec fox has thick fur on the soles of its feet, which help protect it from the hot sand.

Jerboas are the food for another desert mammal, the fennec fox. These small foxes with huge ears get the water they need to survive by eating other desert animals and insects. Fennec foxes also enjoy the sweet fruit of date palm trees found in oases.

The sandfish skink can move quickly through the sand, almost like it is swimming. When threatened, it will bury itself completely under the sand.

The most common creatures found in Kuwait are insects such as grasshoppers, cockroaches, crickets, and scorpions. Reptiles are also common. Reptiles are cold-blooded, which means that their temperature changes with their surroundings. When the sun goes down, their bodies become so chilled that they need to get out into the sun each morning to warm up before they sneak back below the sand. Kuwait's reptiles include lizards, especially geckos and skinks.

Geckos are small insect-eaters found in warm regions throughout the world. The geckos in Kuwait are light brown and gray. Their large eyes don't have movable eyelids. Instead, their eyes are covered with a thin scale that they can see through. This keeps the sand and dust out.

Skinks spend their days searching for food such as fruits and insects. They rest at night under the shelter of sand, stones, or sticks. If a skink needs to make a quick escape, it can lose its tail without any loss of blood. The tail will eventually grow back. Several types of turtles and toads live in Kuwait, too.

Water Animals

Many animals make their home in the waters off Kuwait's coast. King mackerel and barracuda are some of the most common fish. Other marine animals can be dangerous, including dragonish, stonefish, sea snakes, and jellyfish. Stonefish are the most venomous fish on earth. They have large heads and spiny fins that contain the poison. They live in the Gulf's shallow waters near the coast, so someone wading could step on one. Cuts from stonefish can be deadly because of the poison in the spines.

Stonefish are well camouflaged. Their mottled colors make them look just like rocks.

Centuries of Growth

Much of Kuwait is uninhabited and always has been. Even its largest center of population, the Kuwait City area, wasn't settled until the 1600s. In terms of world history, that's not long ago. But archaeologists have discovered evidence of people living in the area that is now Kuwait as far back as 5000 B.C. Very little is known about them.

More is known about the next group to make Kuwait their home. The Dilmun civilization, which was located along the Persian Gulf's western shore, dates to about 4000 B.C. The Dilmun were seafaring people who controlled the water route to India. They carried goods between two of the most important regions of the time, Mesopotamia (in what is now Iraq) and the Indus River valley.

Their civilization was successful until around 1800 B.C., when it was destroyed by invaders. Though the Dilmun continued to trade, they were never again as powerful as they had been. By around 600 B.C., the civilization had been taken over by the Babylonians, who had an empire centered in Mesopotamia.

Opposite: **The Dilmun civilization controlled an empire from their capital in Bahrain.**

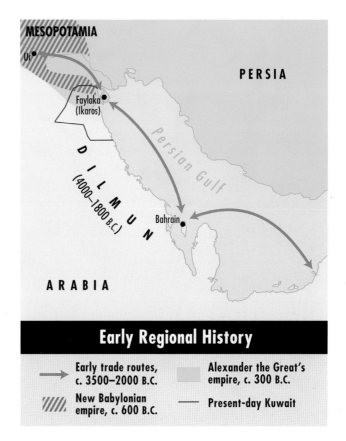

Early Regional History

→ Early trade routes, c. 3500–2000 B.C.

▨ New Babylonian empire, c. 600 B.C.

▧ Alexander the Great's empire, c. 300 B.C.

— Present-day Kuwait

Alexander the Great is considered one of the greatest military commanders in history. His conquests spread Greek culture across a great swath of Asia.

In 326 B.C., a large group of Greek warriors crossed to Faylaka Island. They were members of a scouting party led by Alexander the Great. Alexander was on a mission to create a mighty empire, stretching from Egypt into Persia and India. He sent a group to investigate the Persian Gulf's coastline. Some remained on Faylaka and established a Greek colony, which they called Ikaros after a Greek island in the Aegean Sea. Alexander died before he could accomplish his quest, but the colony flourished. Residents left records of their time on the island through stories inscribed in stone. The stories describe a strong civilization in Kuwait, one that was as advanced as any other at the time. The region was a wealthy center for fishing, trade, and harvesting pearls, gems that form inside oysters.

Little is known about life in Kuwait for the next several hundred years. Few people lived there, and the region was generally quiet and stable. From the third to the fifth centuries A.D., people in the Kuwait region were ruled by the Arab empire of Kinda. Islam reached Kuwait

Early Kuwaiti houses were made from mud-bricks. Some have been uncovered on Faylaka.

in the late 630s. By the end of the ninth century, much of the eastern Arabian Peninsula, including Kuwait, was part of the Carmathian empire, which remained a strong force in the area until around the end of the eleventh century.

After that, Kuwait was under the control of several local amirates. These were tribal groups—large extended families—led by an amir. The amir was something like a chief or a prince. During this time, a port on Kuwait Bay served as the main eastern water entry to the Arabian Peninsula. It was important to traders and other travelers, and controlling it could make a tribe wealthy and powerful. The strongest Arab tribe to emerge during this period was the Bani Khalid, which controlled an area along much of the Gulf's southwestern coast, including Kuwait.

Kuwait's Name

Kuwait's name comes from the Arabic word *kut,* which means "small fort." It's likely that a small fort and perhaps a few tents were the only structures the Bani 'Utub saw when they arrived at the coast, where they settled and founded Kuwait.

This sixteenth-century Ottoman miniature painting shows fishermen in their ships.

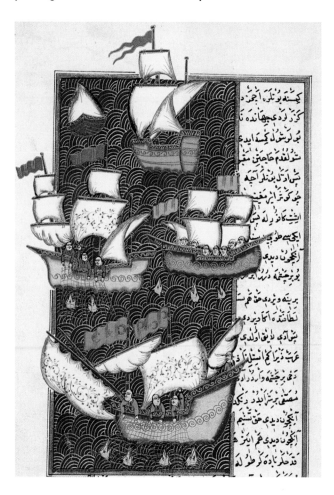

Kuwait Is Founded

Throughout all this history, the land that is now known as Kuwait was not called by that name. Nor did it have the boundaries that it has today. That changed a few centuries later, when the al-Sabah family arrived in Kuwait. Historians are not sure of the exact date. Some point to a letter written by a member of the al-Sabah family about marking the borders to Kuwait in 1613. They see it as proof that the country's origins go back to that year. Others say it was 1670, 1716, or 1722. One thing is certain: the al-Sabah family changed history in Kuwait.

The al-Sabah family was one of about ten families in a larger group known as the Bani 'Utub, which means "the people who moved or trekked." Drought and food shortages had forced the Bani 'Utub to move south from central Arabia. When they arrived in Kuwait, they found little good agricultural land. But they did find water and a natural harbor in Kuwait Bay. Moreover, the region's climate was more moderate than most of the Arabian Peninsula, and the area was not crowded.

They decided to stay and placed themselves under the protection of the ruling tribe, the Bani Khalid. The Bani 'Utub quickly set up a functioning society. Each family had a role to play. The al-Sabah family took care of relations with the Bani Khalid and managed law and order within their community. Another family, the al-Khalifa, took charge of gathering and selling pearls found along the Gulf.

The Kuwait region was peaceful and stable. Permanent homes were built, and businesses flourished. The al-Khalifa family grew as pearlers and moved south along the coast to a better location. They prospered there in what is now the small nation of Bahrain. In time, they took control of Bahrain, and today, they are still the ruling family there. The al-Sabah family did well at maintaining law and order in Kuwait. In the 1750s, the Bani 'Utub gave the al-Sabah family the right to rule the region.

Choosing a Leader

Every shaikh that has ruled Kuwait since 1756 has been from the al-Sabah family. The title of shaikh, or amir, does not necessarily pass from father to oldest son. Rather, each new leader is selected from among several sons, brothers, nephews, and other relatives. The family chooses the man they think is best suited to rule Kuwait, based on his talents and personality. Ahmad al-Jabir al-Sabah (left) became shaikh in 1921, following his uncle's death. He was succeeded by one cousin and then another. Today, one of his sons is shaikh.

Dhows have been used in Kuwait for hundreds of years. Large dhows require crews of thirty men.

Shaikh Sabah ibn Jabir was Kuwait's first leader to emerge from the al-Sabah family. He ruled from 1756 until his death in 1762. Under his rule, Kuwait grew quickly. A Dutch traveler who visited Kuwait in 1756 reported that it had about three hundred small boats in its fleet. Some four years into the new shaikh's reign, the number of boats had increased to more than eight hundred. They were used for fishing, pearling, trade, and defending the coast. Kuwaitis were famous for their *dhows*, sailboats made of teak that were especially strong and swift. The dhows were used in the shipping trade along the coasts of eastern Africa, India, and Arabia.

Land and sea routes connected Kuwait to important trading regions throughout the Middle East. The pearling and fishing industries grew stronger, too. In 1765, German explorer Carsten Niebuhr visited Kuwait. According to Niebuhr, around 70 percent of Kuwait's ten thousand residents left during the summer to work at jobs in pearling or trade.

Outside Attention

Kuwait's increasing prosperity drew the attention of other nations. The Ottomans controlled a vast empire that at its greatest extent stretched across most of southeastern Europe, North Africa, and the Arab world. They claimed Kuwait as part of their empire, but they do not apear to have exercised any power there in the 1700s.

The British had a stronger influence. The Bani 'Utub had always had good relations with the British, and the British began using Kuwait as a base for sending mail across the desert. In the late 1700s, the British East India Company, a trading company, moved its headquarters from Iraq to Kuwait to get away from fighting between the Ottomans and the Persians. Later, in 1795, when the Ottomans threatened to fight for control of Kuwait, the British helped push them back. The British also helped the Kuwaitis fend off attacks by pirates and by the Wahhabis, a fanatical Islamic sect from the center of the Arabian Peninsula.

Rahmah bin Jabir al-Jalahimah was Kuwait's most famous pirate. He typically targeted ships from Kuwait and Bahrain.

Kuwait's relations with the Ottomans improved in the nineteenth century. At that time, the Ottomans ruled much of the Arab Middle East, but not Kuwait. In 1871, the Ottoman governor of Baghdad visited Kuwait and made the Kuwaiti leader, Shaikh Abdullah, a subdistrict governor. But there is no evidence that Kuwait ever paid taxes to the Ottomans or that any Ottoman official was based in Kuwait.

Some were suspicious of the Ottomans' intentions, however. In 1896, the Kuwaiti leader was Shaikh Muhammad.

Ships are unloaded at the British East India Company's docks in London. The company set up a trading post in Kuwait in 1821.

His brother Mubarak did not trust the Ottomans and believed they intended to take over Kuwait. He gathered a small army of followers and murdered his brother the shaikh and another brother, and then made himself ruler.

Despite the bloody beginning to his reign, Mubarak's life was actually quite peaceful. He ruled from 1896 to 1915 and became known as Mubarak the Great. During his reign, Kuwait went from being a shaikhdom, which had no real status in the world, to being a semi-independent state backed by Britain. In 1899, Mubarak signed an agreement with Britain. The British Royal Navy would help protect Kuwait. In return, Kuwait would not deal with any other foreign governments or give away any of its territory without British approval.

The Pearl Trade

For thousands of years, many people in Kuwait depended on pearls for their livelihoods. The pearl trade reached its peak in the early 1900s. Fashionable women throughout Europe and North America wanted pearls. This created an enormous demand.

Pearling was a hard life. Divers attached stones to their feet to help them reach deeper waters and stayed under for as long as two minutes. It was dangerous, too, since sharks and poisonous fish patrolled the waters. But pearling kept Kuwait's economy alive.

When the worldwide economy collapsed in the 1930s, the demand for pearls disappeared. Around the same time, the Japanese developed a way to make cheaper, cultured pearls, and the pearl trade of the Gulf came to an end.

In the 1920s, Ibn Sa'ud, the ruler of Saudi Arabia, sought to take over Kuwait. The British helped to work out a treaty in which Ibn Sa'ud recognized Kuwait's independence. But the Kuwaiti ruler, Shaikh Ahmad al-Jabir al-Sabah, was forced to give up much of the land that he felt was Kuwait's. Ownership of this land, a strip of desert that separates Kuwait from Saudi Arabia, remained in dispute for decades. The land is currently equally divided between Kuwait and Saudi Arabia. Iraq was also making noises about ruling Kuwait. In 1938, Iraq launched a radio campaign claiming that the small country was part of Iraq.

Kuwait changed quickly in the years after oil was discovered there. In Kuwait City, modern buildings were built that towered over the old sections of town.

Drilling for Oil

Soon, foreign countries would have an even greater reason to take over Kuwait, because the search for oil was on. Thick seepage in the desert provided clues that oil might be found below the surface. Only drilling could tell for sure. The Kuwait Oil Company got the right to drill in 1934. This company was a joint venture between the British Petroleum Company and the Gulf Oil Corporation of the United States.

Drilling began in 1936. Within two years, it was clear that Kuwait was sitting atop a major oil field in the desert at Burgan. Drilling and exploration stopped from 1939 to 1945, during World War II. But after the war, further deposits were found at Wafra, North Fawaris, Umm Qadir, al-Managish, Mutriba, and Rawdatayn.

Money was soon flowing into the country as fast as the oil was flowing out. Because the Kuwait Oil Company was owned by two foreign companies, much of the profits went elsewhere, but royalties were paid to the Kuwaiti government. At the time, Kuwait's population was small. The amount of money coming into Kuwait compared with its population was great. Some of the money went to creating more plants to make drinking water and electricity.

When Kuwait's next ruler, Shaikh Abdullah al-Salim al-Sabah, took over in 1950, one of his first acts was to increase the amount of money Kuwait received from oil. In 1951, he and the Kuwait Oil Company agreed to split the profits equally. With the additional money, he built schools and improved Kuwait's educational system so that free education became available for all children. Free health care was also provided in hospitals built with oil money. Programs were set up to care for the elderly, widows, and orphans. Roads, airports, and railways were built to increase trade and create even more profit. Oil enabled Kuwait to become a modern, efficient country, important on the world scene.

Independence

In 1961, Kuwait gained full independence when it ended its protection agreement with Great Britain. Almost immediately, Iraq claimed Kuwait again, stating that Britain had illegally separated it from Iraq. Britain and some Arab nations stepped in to protect Kuwait, and Iraq finally backed down.

In 1962, Shaikh Abdullah approved a Kuwaiti constitution, which had been written by a constitutional assembly. This constitution laid out the system of government and the rights of Kuwaiti citizens. The next year, elections were held to choose Kuwait's National Assembly.

Kuwait settled a long-running dispute with Saudi Arabia in 1966, when the two countries agreed to divide the huge patch of desert separating them, called the Neutral Zone. This area, consisting of 2,200 square miles (5,700 sq km) had long been claimed by both nations. The Treaty of al-'Uqayr, signed in 1969, finally established the boundaries of Kuwait and Saudi Arabia and made each nation responsible for managing its half of the zone. Today, profits from oil production in the zone are shared equally between the two nations.

By this time, about 350,000 Palestinians were living in Kuwait. Palestinians are an Arab people who claim ownership of part of the land that is now occupied by Israel. Whenever Palestinians and Israelis clashed, Kuwait backed the Palestinians.

The Arab-Israeli War broke out in 1973. Kuwait and other Arab oil-producing countries cut back on shipments of oil to Western countries

The Neutral Zone, 1922–1969

Kuwait, 1922

Portion of Neutral Zone given to Kuwait

Portion of Neutral Zone given to Saudi Arabia

—— 1969 border

that supported Israel, including the United States. Halting of shipments like this is called an embargo. The 1973 embargo caused a 70 percent increase in the price of oil. In the United States, consumers faced long lines and high prices at gas stations. In Kuwait, however, higher oil prices brought in more money. This money was used to update roads, factories, ports, and power plants.

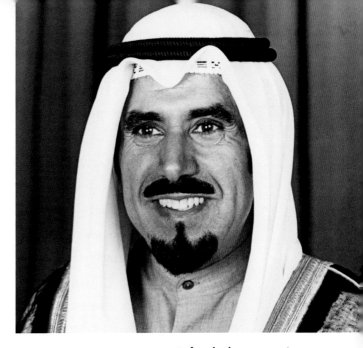

Before he became amir in 1977, Shaikh Jabir al-Ahmad al-Sabah served as Kuwait's finance minister and prime minister. He played a large role in the modernization of Kuwait.

A Difficult Decade

Shaikh Jabir al-Ahmad al-Sabah took over as ruler of Kuwait on the final day of 1977. He held the job until 2006. His understanding of financial matters and knowledge of foreign relations would serve him well during his reign.

From 1980 to 1988, Iraq and Iran fought a war. The war caused havoc for Kuwait as it tried to ship oil out of the country. Though Kuwait said it was not taking sides in the war, it provided financial aid to Iraq. It also allowed ships carrying weapons for Iraq to use the port at Kuwait City.

Iran bombed some of Kuwait's oil wells in 1981. Two years later, Kuwait was bombed again, this time by Islamic Jihad, a militant group with ties to Iran. In 1984, Kuwait blamed Iran when attacks began on Kuwaiti ships in the Persian Gulf. In the years that followed, Kuwaiti ships carrying goods through the Gulf were frequently attacked and robbed. The American and French embassies in Kuwait were also attacked. Then, in 1988, pro-Iranian terrorists hijacked a Kuwait Airways plane.

Kuwait had to do something to protect the country and its ships. It began registering many of its ships as American, Liberian, Russian, or British. Naval escort ships from those nations then protected these ships as they made their way through the Gulf. Kuwait also sought help from other nations to search for buried mines. Further, it forced more than twenty-five thousand Iranians living in Kuwait to leave the country.

Kuwait also faced economic problems during the 1980s. Though the decade began with the country awash in oil profits, things changed quickly. The price of oil dropped sharply in 1985 and 1986, hurting all the oil economies of nations in the Middle East. Kuwait faced further economic troubles when a stock market called the Suq al-Manakh crashed. Many people had invested a great deal of money in the market. Nervous investors tried to cash out of the system, only to find that there weren't enough funds to pay them. Hundreds of people went bankrupt in days. The money they lost was worth more than US$90 billion.

As if these troubles weren't enough, many foreigners were not willing to invest in Kuwait because of the ongoing Iran-Iraq War. They feared the smaller nation could somehow become caught up in the war, too.

The Iran-Iraq War ended as the 1980s drew to a close. Political tensions throughout the Gulf region relaxed. Kuwait's National Assembly had not been allowed to meet during the

Iran-Iraq War, because Shaikh Jabir feared that any opposition might pull the country apart. Now that the war was over, thousands of Kuwaitis marched in the streets, calling for a return to a more democratic form of government. Shaikh Jabir rejected their demands and instead cracked down on those who spoke out against him.

Invasion!

Even though Kuwait gave support to Iraq during the Iran-Iraq War, it was clear that Iraq's leader, Saddam Hussein, was no friend to Kuwait. Hussein claimed that Iraq owned much of the land that Kuwait believed was within its border. He also railed against the wealth of Kuwait. He felt that too many Kuwaitis had fancy cars and glamorous lifestyles. He believed that Kuwaitis were reaping the benefits of oil money that should belong to Iraqis. Many other Iraqis agreed.

In 1990, Saddam Hussein claimed that Kuwait was producing too much oil. He called it "economic warfare" and used it to justify Iraq's invasion of Kuwait.

In July 1990, Hussein accused Kuwait of stealing oil from a field that ran across the border from his country. He also claimed that Kuwait was selling more oil than it had agreed to do. Kuwait denied both charges, and Hussein threatened military action if these disputes were not resolved. Other Arab states tried to work out an agreement, but Hussein would not back down.

Early in the morning on August 2, 1990, some thirty thousand Iraqi troops surged into Kuwait. They came from three directions, so it was nearly impossible for the small Kuwaiti military to put up a fight. The Iraqis quickly made their way to Kuwait City and took over. They captured military bases and the airport. Soon, more Iraqi troops stormed over the border. Kuwait's twenty thousand soldiers were up against an Iraqi force of one hundred thousand. In a few hours, the Iraqis gained control of the entire country.

Iraqi troops rushed to the Kuwaiti palace, hoping to capture Shaikh Jabir. But Kuwait's ruler was a step ahead. Just moments before, he and his family had left the palace, fleeing to safety in neighboring Saudi Arabia.

Trying to Stop Iraq

The United Nations, an international organization that tries to settle disputes between countries, called on Iraq to leave Kuwait. Iraq did not respond. The United States and many other Western nations used embargoes to try to force Iraq out of Kuwait. Iraq could no longer sell oil to some of its biggest customers, and it could no longer purchase food, medicine, and other

The Gulf War, 1990–1991

IRAN
IRAQ
Abdali
KUWAIT
Kuwait Bay
Kuwait City
Al Jahrah
Hawalli
Persian Gulf
SAUDI ARABIA
Al Wafra

→ Iraqi invasion routes, August 1990
→ American invasion routes, February 1991
— Major road
→ Coalition advances, February 1991
++++ Iraqi mine fields
— Present-day boundary

necessary goods. Western nations hoped that the hardships caused by the embargoes would be enough to convince Iraq to leave Kuwait.

More than six hundred Kuwaiti oil wells were set on fire during the Gulf War.

As other nations tried to get Iraq to withdraw, the Kuwaitis were fighting back, too. Though Kuwait's military had been shut down, a small band of citizens formed a resistance group. Under the dark of night, they would climb tall buildings and unfurl banners calling for the Iraqis to leave. They killed some Iraqis and captured others. But their actions did little to stop Hussein and his military.

Meanwhile, Iraqi forces buried land mines throughout the country. They set oil wells on fire, sending flames into the sky. The smoke from these fires was thick and toxic. It filled the atmosphere. Oil spilled out and poisoned the land and the waters of the Gulf.

Kuwaitis Suffer

The people of Kuwait suffered horribly during the invasion. From the beginning, there were arrests, torture, and killings. Many Kuwaitis were randomly pulled off the street and questioned. When university professors were ordered to remove Shaikh Jabir's picture and replace it with Saddam Hussein's, twenty-one were killed for refusing to obey.

Most Kuwaiti citizens managed to avoid death and torture, but they still endured great hardships. Telephone lines

The Tariq Rajab Museum

Jihan Rajab was home alone in the suburb of Hawalli when the Iraqis invaded Kuwait. Her husband, Tariq Sayyid Rajab, was out of the country on business. She was left on her own to protect the priceless items in her basement—the Tariq Rajab Museum.

The museum held a collection of Islamic artworks from around the world, including jewelry, pottery, costumes, miniature paintings, silver, and glass. The Rajabs had spent more than thirty years using their vast knowledge of art and history to gather the treasures.

In 1980, they opened the museum in the basement of their home, and it became a popular attraction for visitors and art lovers from around the world.

When the Iraqis invaded, the museum became a target in their efforts to destroy Kuwaiti history and culture. Jihan Rajab acted quickly. She secretly locked away the finest pieces. In their place, she set out poor-quality items for the invaders to steal and destroy.

Most of the museum's collection was preserved. Today, the museum is open again.

were cut, making communication nearly impossible. Offices and apartment buildings were burned and bombed. Stores were looted. Schools closed and work stopped. Food supplies ran low, causing massive hunger. Kuwaitis were also forced to endure the attempted destruction of their culture. This was part of Hussein's plan—he wanted to rob the Kuwaitis of their national identity. Many Kuwaitis were forced against their will to become Iraqi citizens in order to qualify for medical care and much-needed supplies.

Freedom at Last

In December 1990, four months after the invasion, the United Nations approved the use of military force to get the Iraqis out of Kuwait if they did not leave on their own by January 15, 1991. Hussein did not pull his troops out by the deadline, and bombing began several hours later. The United States and seventeen other nations joined a coalition to force Iraq out of Kuwait.

For five weeks, coalition bombers targeted Iraqi military sites, causing massive destruction. Estimates of how many Iraqis died in the air raids range from ten thousand to one hundred thousand or more. Finally, the coalition ground troops entered the country and finished off the Iraqi military in less than four days. On February 26, 1991, Hussein ordered his troops to leave. Kuwait was free. People danced in the street and ripped down Iraqi flags. Once again, Kuwaiti flags flew over Kuwait.

After putting out an oil well fire, the well must be capped. Here, men struggle to cap a well amid a shower of oil.

Rebuilding the Nation

There was plenty of work to be done to get Kuwait back into shape. The rebuilding projects ahead were massive.

First on the agenda was repairing the utilities: the water, electricity, gas, and phone lines. Roads were rebuilt quickly, too. Next came schools, hospitals, and government buildings as wells as shops and homes. Before anything could be built, though, tons of rubble had to be cleared away.

The Iraqis had set hundreds of oil wells on fire. Putting out these fires was an incredible challenge, since an unending supply of oil fueled the fires.

Thousands of specialists from more than thirty-five countries worked on the task. Though experts had estimated it would take years to put out the flames, remarkably, they were all out in less than nine months.

Moving Forward

In the years since the Iraqi invasion, Kuwait's focus has been on maintaining stability. This has been a great challenge.

Returning to a normal, stable life after the brutal Iraqi occupation was difficult. Buildings were repaired, but people also had to feel that life was back to normal. It was helpful

U.S. Marines march through the Kuwaiti desert prior to the U.S. invasion of Iraq in 2003. The United States has four military bases in Kuwait.

when, in 1992, Shaikh Jabir once again allowed the National Assembly to meet. This gave people more control over their government.

Another challenge to Kuwait's stability has been its location. The country is tucked into a dangerous spot in the world, amid some very unstable neighbors.

In 2003, the United States invaded Iraq, and the situation there remains extremely volatile. The U.S. military has several bases in Kuwait. Nearby Iran may be working toward building nuclear weapons. In the middle of all this, tiny Kuwait is trying to balance its friendship with the United States and its need for American protection with the fact that the United States is hated by many people in the Gulf region and in the Middle East as a whole.

In January 2006, Kuwait faced a new challenge to its stability when Shaikh Jabir passed away. He had been in power nearly thirty years. Following tradition, the crown prince, Shaikh Sa'd al-Abdullah al-Sabah, immediately took over as amir. But he was seventy-six years old and in poor health. So the National Assembly took the highly unusual step of removing him from power. He was replaced by Shaikh al-Sabah al-Ahmad al-Sabah, seventy-seven, who was in better health. Shaikh Sabah had been the nation's prime minister.

The days following the death of Shaikh Jabir were confusing. But through it all, Kuwaitis were calm. There was no threat of a hostile takeover or any other major change to the nation's politics. Kuwait remained stable, a sure sign that its government is strong.

Governing the Nation

THE CURRENT GOVERNMENT IN KUWAIT REACHES BACK to 1756, when a member of the al-Sabah family first became ruler of the amirate. Each leader, or amir, selects the member of the family who will become the crown prince and, eventually, the next amir.

The government is led by the prime minister, who is also a member of the al-Sabah family. The prime minister is appointed by the amir. Government decisions are made by a cabinet known as the Council of Ministers, who are appointed by the prime minister. Several ministers are members of the al-Sabah family.

Opposite: **A clock tower rises above the municipal building in Kuwait City.**

The Kuwaiti amir lives in Sief Palace in Kuwait City.

Shaikh Jabir al-Ahmad al-Sabah

Shaikh Jabir al-Ahmad al-Sabah served as Kuwait's ruler from 1977 to 2006, guiding the country during some of its most troubled times. Born in Kuwait City in 1928, he was the son of Shaikh Ahmad al-Jabir al-Sabah. Shaikh Jabir was educated at private schools in Kuwait, studying Arabic, English, science, and religion. He was forty-nine when he succeeded his cousin as amir.

Shaikh Jabir is remembered by many as an intelligent and powerful yet humble man. His palace in Kuwait, though large, was rather plain. He often ate simple meals of bread and yogurt. Children, the elderly, and the disabled got special attention from him, and he liked spending time with ordinary people in his country. He had to cut down on public appearances, though, after 1985, when he was nearly killed by a suicide bomber who drove a car into a royal procession.

Shaikh Jabir's death in January 2006 set off a period of mourning throughout the country. Many world leaders attended his funeral, including the president of Iraq and the king of Saudi Arabia. More than ten thousand Kuwaitis were on hand to honor him as he was lowered into his grave.

The National Assembly

Kuwait's parliament, known as the National Assembly, consists of fifty people. Members of the National Assembly, who must be at least thirty years old, are elected to four-year terms. The National Assembly considers the decisions and laws made by the Council of Ministers and can approve or overturn them.

The amir holds considerable power over the National Assembly. He may decide that he doesn't like a law that has been passed and can reject it. He also has the authority to

The National Assembly building is one of the most striking buildings in Kuwait. Its shape is meant to recall that of a Bedouin tent.

completely shut down, or dissolve, the National Assembly. This has happened three times during Kuwait's history. Still, having the parliament gives Kuwaitis much closer ties to their government than people in most Gulf nations have. They have a way to contact their elected officials and make their views heard.

Only Kuwaiti citizens who are at least twenty-one years old may vote. Most citizens are people whose ancestors lived in Kuwait in 1920. People who have been naturalized citizens for at least thirty years also may vote. (A naturalized citizen is someone who moves to a new nation and chooses to take on that nationality.) Huge numbers of people who live in Kuwait

NATIONAL GOVERNMENT OF KUWAIT

Amir

Executive Branch

PRIME MINISTER

COUNCIL OF MINISTERS

Legislative Branch

NATIONAL ASSEMBLY

Judicial Branch

COURT OF CASSATION

COURT OF APPEALS

COURTS OF FIRST INSTANCE

A Woman in the Cabinet

In June 2005, Kuwait's ruler appointed the first female member of the Council of Ministers. Mas'uma al-Mubarak is a former political science teacher at Kuwait University. She is also a newspaper columnist and women's rights advocate. She holds a doctorate in international relations from the University of Colorado in Denver. On the cabinet, al-Mubarak was placed in charge of planning and administrative development.

Until 2005, women could not serve on the cabinet because women were not allowed to vote. Kuwaiti law states that all cabinet members must be able to vote. After being appointed, al-Mubarak said, "This is a breakthrough for us as Kuwaiti women, for us as Kuwaitis, and for Kuwait itself."

have moved there from other countries. They are not citizens and thus cannot vote. Women in Kuwait were only granted the right to vote in 2005.

The Judicial System

Kuwait has two separate court systems. One is secular, or non-religious, and the other is Islamic.

Secular courts try civil cases, such as those involving business disputes, and criminal cases. These courts are called Courts of First Instance. If a person is not satisfied with the verdict in this court, he or she has the right to take the case to the Court of Appeals. This court will examine the verdict and decide if the law was applied properly. If a person still isn't

Trials are held at the Justice Palace in Kuwait City.

satisfied, the Court of Cassation may consider the case. This is the highest court in Kuwait.

Family cases are tried in the Islamic court system. This court system has two separate sets of courts, which are based on the two main sects of Islam, Sunni and Shi'i. Though men and women are equal in secular courts, in Islamic courts the testimony of one man is equal to the testimony of two women.

Kuwait's Flag

Kuwait's flag is twice as long as it is wide. On the left is a black trapezoid shape. Alongside it are three stripes of green, white, and red. Green symbolizes Islam, while white represents Kuwait's achievements. The future is symbolized by red, and black represents victory on the battlefield.

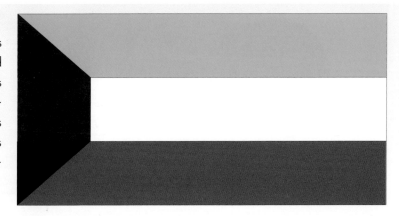

Unlike in Saudi Arabia, women in Kuwait are allowed to drive. They also gained the right to vote in 2005.

Kuwait's citizens enjoy greater personal freedoms than those people living in many other countries in the region. They

can live anywhere in Kuwait that they please, and they can travel abroad. They have freedom of speech and are allowed to express their opinions on a variety of subjects, even if the government disagrees.

Women in Kuwait enjoy more freedoms than women in some other Middle Eastern countries. They can vote, and girls are educated just as boys in Kuwait are. Kuwaiti women may dress as they choose.

But Kuwaiti women do face some restrictions. As is the case elsewhere in the Muslim world, if a Muslim woman wishes to marry a non-Muslim man, he must first convert to Islam. A Muslim man is free, however, to marry a woman who is not Muslim. An unmarried woman may get a passport and travel outside Kuwait whenever she wishes. A married woman must get her husband's permission to obtain a passport to leave the country.

Kuwait's laws about inheriting property come from Islamic law. They differ depending on the type of Islam practiced. A Shi'i woman may inherit all her husband's property if he has no sons. A Sunni woman, however, must share the property with her male relatives.

Kuwait's National Anthem

Kuwait's national anthem, "Al-Nashid al-Watani," was adopted in 1978. It was written by the poet Ahmad Mashari al-Adwani. Ibrahim al-Sula composed the music.

English translation

> Kuwait, Kuwait, Kuwait,
> My country,
> In peace live, in dignity,
> Your face bright,
> Your face bright,
> Your face bright with majesty,
> Kuwait, Kuwait, Kuwait,
> My country.
> Oh cradle of ancestry,
> Who put down its memory,
> With everlasting symmetry,
> Showing all eternity,
> Those Arabs were Heavenly,
> Kuwait, Kuwait, Kuwait,
> My country.

Kuwait City: Did You Know This?

Kuwait City, the national capital, is located on land that juts out into Kuwait Bay. Though the city has only 32,600 residents, the metropolitan area surrounding the city is home to more than 1.7 million people. Locals call it *al-Dira,* or "the City." Most government buildings are located in Kuwait City, as are the headquarters of nearly all Kuwait's major businesses.

The city's architecture is a mix of old and new. The oldest homes and public buildings, constructed before the oil boom, are usually simple structures. Some are decorated with paintings and mosaics. One of the oldest examples open to the public is Sadu House. Today, the building serves as a museum dedicated to preserving Kuwait's traditional Bedouin crafts, especially weaving.

After oil was found, the country suddenly became wealthy, and construction began on a grand scale. Modern office towers and enormous buildings became the norm. The Kuwait Towers are a good example. These three towers, built in 1979, dominate the skyline and are a symbol of the city. Two of these narrow, needle-like towers each pierce a large globe and are water storage facilities. One of these towers also has a smaller globe on top that houses restaurants, shops, and an observation deck. The third tower illuminates the other two.

The Grand Mosque is another notable building in Kuwait City. The huge building, which opened in 1986, is made of concrete and stone. It has a large central dome, 85 feet (26 m) across and 141 feet (43 m) tall, and is decorated throughout with ornate Islamic designs. It is large enough to hold ten thousand worshippers.

The National Assembly Building is a distinctive white building with sloping sides and a sweeping roof. It was designed to resemble a Bedouin tent.

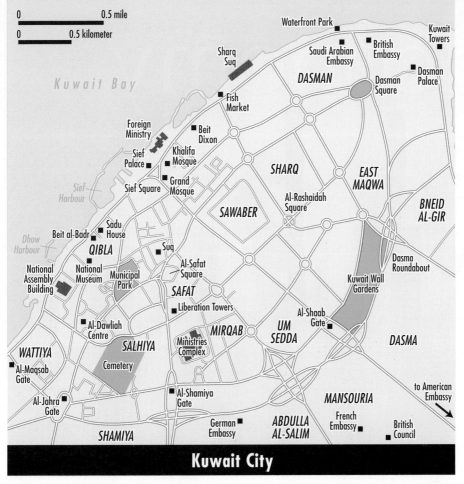

Kuwait City

An Oil Economy

OIL DOMINATES KUWAIT'S ECONOMY. THERE IS LITTLE economic activity in the country that does not involve oil in some way.

Kuwait holds 10 percent of the world's oil reserves—about 99 billion barrels, according to the Kuwaiti government. This means that if production continues at current rates, it should last more than one hundred years. There is some dispute, however, about whether this estimate is accurate. Some experts estimate that Kuwait's reserves are only about half of the official government claim.

Opposite: **Oil refineries dot the Kuwaiti landscape.**

Huge amounts of oil escaped from burning wells during the Gulf War. This oil collected into more than three hundred lakes.

Weights and Measures

Kuwait uses the metric system of weights and measures. The basic unit of distance is the meter, which equals 39.4 inches. The basic unit of weight is the kilogram, which equals 2.2 pounds.

Kuwait also has natural gas. In some parts of the world, natural gas is mixed with crude oil in the same reserves. This is called associated gas. In other areas, it occurs alone. The bulk of gas in Kuwait is associated gas.

It is difficult to transport natural gas efficiently, so Kuwaiti officials are working to make greater use of it at home. They expect to switch from oil to natural gas for their own electricity production and desalination plants. This should free up more oil for export.

Oil pipelines run across vast stretches of Kuwaiti desert.

Kuwait's Currency

The basic unit of the Kuwaiti money is the dinar, which is divided into 1,000 fils. In 2006, 1 Kuwaiti dinar was equal to 3.46 U.S. dollars, and 1 U.S. dollar was equal to .29 dinar.

Kuwait frequently changes the art on its money. A 1 dinar note from 2001 shows the port of Kuwait. Two men are in the foreground, one waving a Kuwaiti flag, while a dhow sails in the harbor. Another recent 1 dinar note shows ships in a busy industrial port on the front. On the back is a drawing of the Kuwait Towers.

Oil and related products make up about 90 percent of Kuwait's exports. Though Kuwait makes most of its income from the sale of crude oil, the country is working to diversify the type of work it does in the oil industry. Kuwait is now home to businesses that refine, market, and distribute oil to other countries around the world. The government is offering financial help to encourage this development.

Investing for the Future

Another major source of revenue for Kuwait is the interest earned on investments the government has made in other countries. Even this is related to oil, since the amount invested each year is equal to 10 percent of the nation's oil revenue.

These investments are called the Fund for Future Generations. The fund, which began in 1976, was extremely

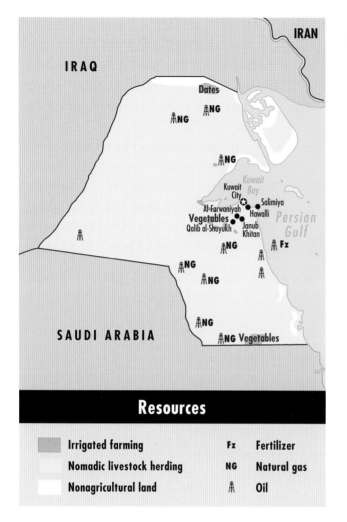

IRAN

IRAQ

Dates

Kuwait Bay

Kuwait City

Salimiya

Al-Farwaniyah

Hawalli

Vegetables

Qalib al-Shuyukh

Janub Khitan

Persian Gulf

Fz

SAUDI ARABIA

NG Vegetables

Resources

Irrigated farming		Fz	Fertilizer
Nomadic livestock herding		NG	Natural gas
Nonagricultural land		A	Oil

helpful during the Iraqi invasion. The Iraqis stole much of the wealth in Kuwait, but the fund's investments were held, untouched, abroad. The money helped support some of the Kuwaitis who fled the country for their safety. The fund also paid for some of the costs of the military response and, later, made it possible to rebuild quickly. Prior to the 1990 invasion, the Fund for Future Generations was worth about US$100 billion. But within two years it was down to US$40 billion.

The government quickly began adding to the total fund again. Today, the stated purpose of the fund is to build a reserve of money that will provide for the country when, someday, its oil reserves are gone.

Farming and Fishing

Kuwait has dry, poor soil, so agriculture has never been a big part of the country's economy. Only about 1 percent of the land is suitable for farming. Most of the farmland is near the southern border, where there is a small natural water supply. The main crops grown there are tomatoes, potatoes, radishes, cucumbers, melons, and cereal grains. The amount of food grown in southern Kuwait is not nearly enough to feed the country. Almost all the fruit, vegetables, grains, dairy products, and meat that Kuwaitis eat every day is imported from other countries. Some milk is produced in Kuwait, and some farmers raise chickens, sheep, and goats.

Vegetables, such as eggplants, grow in southern Kuwait.

What Kuwait Grows, Makes, and Mines

Agriculture (2004)

Chicken	41,745 metric tons
Milk	40,000 metric tons
Tomatoes	36,000 metric tons
Potatoes	33,000 metric tons

Manufacturing Exports (2004)

Cement	2,145,000 metric tons
Fertilizer	255,300 metric tons

Mining

Crude oil (2005)	806 million barrels per day
Natural gas (2004)	8.7 billion cubic meters

Kuwaiti fishermen bring in about 9,000 metric tons of fish and shrimp each year. All of the fish are eaten in Kuwait, but some of the shrimp are exported.

Fishing is also a small part of the Kuwaiti economy. Fishermen bring in catches of shad, grouper, mullet, snapper, and shrimp. Seafood is an important part of the Kuwaiti diet, so it is in great demand. Because Kuwait's fishing industry provides only about 25 percent of the seafood that people want, a good deal of seafood is imported.

Manufacturing plays a minor role in Kuwait's economy. Bricks, aluminum windows and doors, fertilizer, and cement are the main items manufactured in Kuwait. Most of the factories are in the suburbs surrounding Kuwait City. These factories were damaged during the Iraqi invasion, but they have been rebuilt. The government has helped manufacturing to grow by providing loans and offering low-cost electricity to keep the factories running.

After the end of the Gulf War, Kuwait quickly rebuilt its many damaged buildings. The government tried to make many of the buildings look exactly as they had before.

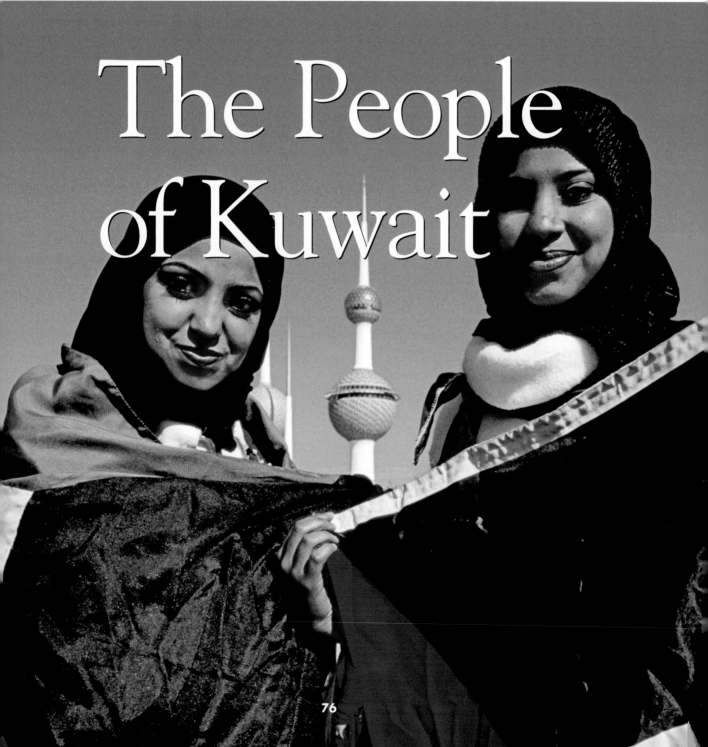

The People of Kuwait

NOTHING IS MORE IMPORTANT TO A KUWAITI THAN his or her family. In Kuwait, as in many Arab nations, the large, extended family unit forms the main focus for social life. When Kuwaitis celebrate, when they relax, when they eat, when they worship—it is almost always with members of their family.

Kuwaitis also rely on their family members. When Kuwaitis are in trouble, they can usually count on relatives to help

Opposite: **Girls with Kuwaiti flags wait to meet their country's leader.**

A Kuwaiti family enjoys a picnic at the beach.

Population of Major Cities (2005)

Qalib al-Shuyukh	179,264
Salimiya	145,328
Hawalli	106,992
Janub Khitan	92,646
al-Farwaniyah	83,544

them out. When they grow old, younger family members will provide support. But relying so heavily on family sometimes prevents Kuwaitis from reaching out to people who are not relatives. It keeps them somewhat isolated from others, and members of different social classes rarely interact.

Kuwaitis live an average of seventy-seven years. Older people typically live with one of their children.

A sheep vendor sits on a street in Kuwait City. Many of the sheep in Kuwait are imported from Australia.

Levels of Society

Kuwaiti society is divided into several levels. The first three levels consist of Kuwaiti citizens. At the top are members of the ruling family. Next are those whose ancestors were the merchants who founded the larger settlements in early Kuwait. These settlements grew into the country's major urban centers. The last are the descendants of Kuwait's early desert dwellers, farmers, and fishermen. This group began to merge with the other Kuwaitis in the 1940s. At that time, many rural people began moving to the cities to work in the oil industry.

The People of Kuwait **79**

Persons per square mile		Persons per square kilometer	
130–259		50–99	
3–24		1–9	
fewer than 3		fewer than 1	

A majority of the people in Kuwait are foreigners who moved to the country to find work. Most immigrants to Kuwait are male.

Kuwait also has two classes of noncitizens: Arabs from other countries and non-Arabs from other countries. Foreigners make up more than half of the people living in Kuwait. Many came to this wealthy Gulf nation to find jobs. Nearly 80 percent of the working people in the country are non-Kuwaitis. The non-Arabs in Kuwait are mostly from India, Pakistan, and Iran.

The Bidun

The Bedouin are the desert people of the Middle East. In the past, the Bedouin were nomadic. They traveled about the desert paying no attention to the borders between countries. But now some Bedouin are having a hard time gaining acceptance as citizens in Kuwait. In 1985, the Kuwaiti government refused to grant full citizenship to people who could not prove that their families were longtime residents of Kuwait. Because of their nomadic traditions, many Bedouin could not provide such proof. They became "Bidun," people without any official citizenship. In Arabic, the word *bidun* means "without."

Kuwait's Ethnic Breakdown

Kuwaiti	45%
Other Arab	35%
South Asian	9%
Iranian	4%
Other	7%

The lives of Bedouin are a mix of the traditional and the modern. Bedouin may travel about on camels, but they also chat on cell phones.

In 2000, Bidun residents of Kuwait were forced to give up their claims to citizenship in exchange for the right to continue living in the country. Today, Kuwait is home to more than one hundred thousand Bidun. They don't receive the same quality of education and health care that Kuwaiti citizens get. Many are without jobs, and they are not allowed to travel. Kuwaiti officials agree that this is a serious problem, but so far they haven't come up with a way to solve it.

Bedouin families tend to have more children than non-Bedouin Kuwaitis. Because they are not citizens, Bedouin children cannot enroll in public schools.

Many Palestinians supported Iraq's invasion of Kuwait in 1990. In 2004, Palestinian leader Mahmoud Abbas (center) apologized to Kuwaitis for this.

A Minority in Their Own Country

Before the Iraqi invasion of 1990, only about 25 percent of the people living in Kuwait were citizens. Following the invasion, the government made an effort to raise the percentage of Kuwaitis. It expelled more than four hundred thousand Palestinians from Kuwait because some Palestinian leaders had supported the Iraqi invasion. The Kuwaitis also lowered the number of other foreigners in the country. By 2006, Kuwaitis made up about 45 percent of the population.

The Arabic Alphabet

a	ا	d*	ض
b	ب	t*	ط
t	ت	z*	ظ
th	ث	pause	ع
g	ج	gh	غ
h	ح	f	ف
kh	خ	q	ق
d	د	k	ك
dh	ذ	l	ل
r	ر	m	م
z	ز	n	ن
s	س	h	ه
sh	ش	w	و
s*	ص	y	ي

*Harder sounds

Above right: **Road signs in Kuwait use both Arabic and English.**

The Arabic Language

Arabic is Kuwait's official language, but English is widely used. Road signs are printed in both languages, and most business is conducted the same way. Still, Kuwaitis appreciate it when visitors make the effort to learn at least a few Arabic phrases.

Written Arabic reads from right to left, the opposite of English. The letters are cursive, so each letter in a word flows into those around it. The Arabic alphabet has twenty-eight letters, all consonants. Three short vowel sounds are represented by symbols written above or below the letters. Each consonant can be written in three different ways, depending on whether it comes at the beginning, middle, or end of a word.

Common Arabic Words and Phrases

Insha'allah	God willing
Salâm alaykum	Peace be with you
Shukran	Thank you
Asif	I am sorry
Wáalid	Father
Wáalidah	Mother
Akh	Brother
Ukht	Sister
Jáahil	Child

Arabic is full of flowing, curved letters. Calligraphy— the art of writing—is a highly respected art form in Kuwait and other Arab nations.

Body Language and Customs

Kuwaitis are typically friendly and warm. They are known for their generosity and patience, and they will not show anger outwardly. In fact, it is considered very poor form to get upset in public in a social or business setting.

Kuwaiti men shake hands frequently, usually with everyone in a room when entering and when leaving. While talking, Kuwaitis stand closer together than is typical in the West.

In Kuwait, men often kiss each other on the cheek as a greeting. The same is true throughout most of the Arab world.

They often sit nearer to each other as well. To Kuwaitis, this closeness is simply a demonstration of friendship. Men and women, though, do not even shake hands. This is considered inappropriate.

Other things are also not done. Kuwaitis don't beckon for someone with their index finger—this shows contempt. Instead, they hold out their right hand, palm down, and curl their fingers in toward themselves. In addition, the bottoms of the feet should never be pointed toward another person. And it is impolite to pass in front of someone who is praying.

Kuwaitis have a good deal of contact with foreigners, so they are typically not too strict about following these rules. But they do appreciate it when they feel that their culture is respected.

The body language of Kuwaitis shows the importance of being open and friendly in the culture. Kuwaitis typically sit and stand close to one another.

The Word of God

This man is on his way to pray at a mosque in Kuwait City. On Fridays, Muslims gather for prayer at mosques.

I T IS NEARLY IMPOSSIBLE TO SEPARATE RELIGION FROM THE rest of life in Kuwait. Religion plays a strong part in Kuwaiti culture, affecting topics as different as art, food, and social interactions.

Islam is Kuwait's official religion. Of the more than 2.3 million people living in Kuwait, about 1.95 million are Muslim. Nearly all Kuwaiti citizens are Muslim. About 65 percent of the Muslim population are Sunnis, including the ruling family. The remaining 35 percent are Shi'is.

Opposite: **Most mosques include a tall, slender tower called a minaret.**

The Word of God   **89**

Religions of Kuwait

Sunni Muslim	55%
Shi'i Muslim	30%
Other	15%

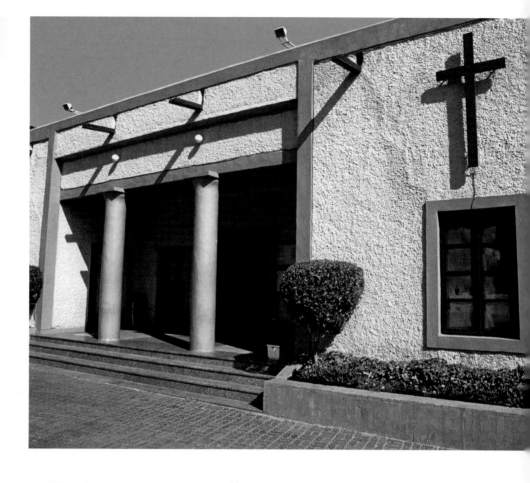

The National Evangelical Church has about twenty thousand members. They come from fifteen different nations.

The Kuwaiti government allows members of other religions to practice their faith. Though no Kuwaiti citizens are Christians, about 100,000 Roman Catholics live in Kuwait, along with 150,000 people who belong to other Christian groups. This includes evangelical churches, Greek Orthodox, and the Church of Jesus Christ of Latter-day Saints (Mormons). In addition, Kuwait is home to about 100,000 Hindus as well as some Sikhs and Baha'is. In general, the country has a reputation in the region for religious tolerance, and people of different faiths get along.

The Prophet Muhammad

The Prophet Muhammad was born in A.D. 570 in Mecca, which is now part of Saudi Arabia. Muhammad's parents died when he was a child. He grew up to become a camel driver and trader, with a wife and children.

Muslims believe that when Muhammad was about forty years old, he was visited by the angel Gabriel who revealed to him the "word of God." The word of God explained how people should live, what they should believe, and how they should worship. The revelations supposedly continued for the rest of Muhammad's life. These messages from God were collected in a book called the Qur'an, the Muslims' holy book.

Muhammad felt it was his responsibility to share the word of God with the people around him. Beginning in 613, he began speaking out about his visions. But the people of Mecca did not accept his message, and he attracted only a few dozen followers. Most people already had their own beliefs and they were angry with Muhammad for attacking the idols they worshipped. Muhammad also taught that people should help the poor. It was wrong, he declared, to make a lot of money by charging high interest on loans. Money lenders and other wealthy people didn't want to hear this. When Muhammad's life was threatened by those who opposed his message, he left Mecca. He and his followers moved to the nearby town of Medina in a journey now known as the Hijra, or "Migration." This was in 622, which became year 1 on the Muslim calendar.

In Medina, people were much more open to Muhammad's teachings. In a few years, he had thousands of followers. He gathered some ten thousand soldiers in 630 and led them back to Mecca. There, they destroyed the idols and called the people to Islam. Mecca was ready to follow him. Muhammad died just two years later, but Islam continued to thrive.

History of Islam

The word *Islam* means "[the act of] submission to the will of God." The word *Muslim* means "one who submits to the will of God." God is called Allah in Arabic.

Muslims believe that Muhammad began receiving revelations from God in around A.D. 610. Within two decades, Islam had spread across Arabia. In ten more years, it had spread throughout much of the Middle East. Within a hundred years, the faith had spread westward to Spain and eastward to

The Islamic Calendar

The Islamic calendar is sometimes called the Hijri calendar. It begins with the day in 622 when Muhammad left Mecca for Medina.

The Islamic calendar is a lunar calendar, meaning it is tied to the phases of the moon. A month is the period of time between two new moons.

The Islamic calendar has 354 days. The Western calendar, based on the solar year, has 365 days.

Kuwaitis typically use the Western calendar for business. But religious holidays are based on the Islamic calendar, so Kuwaitis are also mindful of it.

western India. By the time the al-Sabah family arrived in Kuwait in the early 1600s, Islam had been long established as the major religion throughout the Gulf region for a thousand years.

In this picture from 1719, Muslim pilgrims travel to Medina, where Muhammad is buried.

Teachings of Islam

Allah is the same God that Christians and Jews worship, and many of the teachings in Islam, Christianity, and Judaism are similar. Islam also accepts the teachings of many of the Old Testament prophets and recognizes their place in the Islamic tradition. Muslims believe that Jesus too was a prophet. But beacuse of their belief in the one-ness of God, they do not accept that he was the son of God, as Christians do. Muhammad's teachings, Muslims believe, are the most complete and accurate messages from God. They also believe that Muhammad was the last prophet. Thus, the Qur'an is God's final revelation to mankind.

Muslims are supposed to dress modestly. For girls, that often means covering the hair and wearing clothing that hides the shape of the body.

Kuwait City's Grand Mosque is the largest mosque in the country. It can hold more than ten thousand worshippers at one time.

The Five Pillars of Islam

Faithful Muslims follow what are called the Five Pillars of Islam. Just as the pillars of a building give it strength and structure, so, too, do the Five Pillars of Islam give structure to the lives of Muslims.

The first pillar of Islam is *shahada*, or witnessing. Muslims must make a public statement of faith. They pronounce a verse in Arabic that translates: "I bear witness that there is no God but Allah and I bear witness that Muhammad is His messenger."

The second pillar is *salat*. This is the requirement that Muslims pray five times a day—at dawn, midday, midafternoon, sunset, and evening. The noon prayer on Fridays is usually done in a mosque, or a house of worship. At other times, the prayers can take place anywhere—home, school, or work. Muslims must purify themselves by washing their face, neck, hands, arms, and feet before praying. Then they kneel, bowing low to the ground as a way to show submission to Allah. They always pray facing the holy city of Mecca.

The third pillar, *zakat*, requires that Muslims give alms, or donations, to the poor. Muslims are expected to give 2.5 percent of their income. If they can afford to give more, this is considered a good deed.

During the holy month of Ramadan, the ninth month of the Islamic calendar, Muslims observe the fourth pillar, *sawm*, or fasting. During Ramadan, Muslims do not eat, drink,

At most mosques, men and women pray in separate areas.

or smoke during daylight hours. This takes a good deal of discipline. To Muslims, however, it is an act of worship that instills in them a sense of devotion, willpower, moderation, maturity, and unity. Only pregnant women, travelers, and old and young people need not observe this rule.

The final pillar is the performance of the *hajj.* This is the requirement that all Muslims make a pilgrimage, or visit, to Mecca at least once in their lifetimes, if at all possible. In Mecca, the pilgrims wear white robes and pray at the Great Mosque. While praying, they walk seven times around the Ka'ba, a shrine holding the black stone that Muslims believe God gave to the prophet Abraham. Millions of Muslims take part in the hajj each year during the Islamic month of Dhu al-Hijjah, making it the world's largest annual religious gathering.

Besides the Five Pillars, many Muslims also follow the laws set down in the Qur'an. Islam prohibits Muslims from killing, stealing, lying, and drinking alcohol. They are instructed to dress and behave with modesty and to be charitable and fair. Muslims are not allowed to eat pork or the meat of any animal that died of natural causes. Muslim men may marry Christian, Jewish, or Muslim women, but Muslim women are only allowed to marry Muslim men.

Types of Islam

After Muhammad died, his followers disagreed about who should take over as caliph, or the leader of the faith. Islam split into two branches, or sects, Sunni and Shi'i. In Kuwait,

Worshippers gather for the first day of 'Id al-Adha. The celebration lasts three days.

most Muslims, including the ruling family, are Sunni. This reflects the situation in the rest of the Islamic world, where about 85 percent of Muslims are Sunni. The Kuwaiti government gives Shi'is full freedom to worship as they choose, but the number of mosques they may build is limited. There are only about 40 Shi'i mosques in Kuwait, compared with more than 1,300 Sunni mosques.

Religious Holidays

Muslims in Kuwait observe several religious holidays throughout the year. Among them are Ramadan, the month of fasting from sunrise to sunset. Each evening at sunset, families come together for their meal, called *iftar*. The evenings during Ramadan are a busy time for Muslims. They often gather to socialize and conduct business.

At the end of Ramadan, Kuwaitis celebrate 'Id al-Fitr, a joyful three-day celebration. They prepare delicious meals, wear new clothes, buy gifts for their children, and give money to the poor. Fireworks often light up the night sky.

'Id al-Adha, the Feast of Sacrifice, takes place each year at the end of the hajj. At this time, Muslims recall how the prophet Abraham was ready to sacrifice his only son, Isaac, to obey God. Kuwaitis sacrifice a sheep and prepare the meat. They use some for a feast for themselves and share the rest with friends and the poor. During this three-day holiday, businesses remain closed.

The Prophet's birthday, Mawlid al-Nabi, is a lively holiday during the third month, Rabi' al-Awwal. It is celebrated with feasting and dancing late into the night.

Al-Isra w'al-Mi'raj marks the night on which Muslims believe that Muhammad ascended a gold and silver staircase to heaven. Many Muslims spend the day in prayer and fasting.

Kuwaitis line up to sacrifice sheep during 'Id al-Adha. The festival also includes giving gifts to children.

Culture and Sports

A NATION'S ART AND CULTURE REFLECT ITS PEOPLE and their history. Kuwait is no different. Its art and culture are well grounded in the long traditions of Islam and the Arab world. They are also influenced by Kuwait's wealth since the oil boom and the country's devastation and rebuilding after the Iraqi invasion. These varied factors influence Kuwait's art, film, and music.

Opposite: **A craftsman carves a miniature dhow, the traditional boat used by Kuwaitis.**

Kuwait is proud of its bold, modern architecture such as the Stock Exchange Building.

Art

Muslims believe that Allah is the only creator of life. Making images of living things trespasses on Allah's role as creator, so Kuwaiti artists rarely make art showing humans or animals. Islamic art typically uses intricate geometric shapes and patterns. Any people, animals, or plants found in Islamic art are highly stylized and abstract. They do not look realistic. This abstract style is found in older works, such as woven rugs and blankets, printed books, and vases and dishes. Today, it is also seen in architecture, metal items such as trays, and jewelry.

These tiles from a mosque in Kuwait are decorated with plant images. People and animals are seldom shown in Kuwaiti art.

Kuwait's Bedouin are known for their woven textiles incorporating Islamic designs. Called *al-sadu*, the weaving process is one of Kuwait's oldest crafts. With modern equipment, people no longer need to weave their own wool fabric. But a group called the al-Sadu Society was formed in 1979 to preserve the craft. The artists create cloaks, blankets, rugs, and cushions—items that were once made by the Bedouin, who used them as they traveled about the desert.

The al-Sadu Society honors the art of Bedouin weaving. Bedouin designs are simpler than those found in much of the Muslim world.

This painting commemorates the Iraqi invasion of Kuwait. It includes figures, but not realistic ones.

Most modern Kuwaiti paintings are not in the style of traditional Islamic art. Still, they avoid showing realistic people, plants, and animals. Some use swirls of strong color to show emotions and movement. Symbols and abstract shapes and figures are also common.

The Kuwaiti government encourages modern artists. It began arts education in the schools in the 1950s. The National Council for Culture, Arts, and Letters, established in 1973, promotes art. Not only does it support new artists, but it works to revive Kuwait's traditional arts and crafts, such as leatherwork, loom weaving, and palm-frond basket weaving.

The National Museum

Kuwait's National Museum, located in Kuwait City, is renowned for its outstanding collection of Islamic art. The museum opened in the 1950s in a nineteenth-century house. It soon outgrew these surroundings as researchers and archaeologists began to uncover more artifacts from Kuwait's past. With its oil income, Kuwait was able to build a larger museum in 1983, adding two buildings.

One of the buidings housed the Dar al-Athar al-Islamiyyah (DAI), or House of Islamic Antiquities. The DAI displays Islamic artwork from around the world. The collection includes items such as fourteenth-century metal candlesticks and glasswork from the seventeenth century. It is one of the most valuable collections of Islamic art in the world.

Many people feared that pieces from the DAI collection would be destroyed when the Iraqi army stormed into Kuwait in 1990. Shortly after the invasion, Iraqis looted the museum. Nearly all the pieces were returned after the war, though some were damaged. The museum buildings were destroyed in the war. They have not been repaired. This serves as a stark reminder of the occupation. Today, only a small portion of the museum is open to the public.

Cinema

Kuwait's film history dates back to 1930. A documentary, *Sons of Sinbad*, was shot in Kuwait that year, though it was made by foreigners. A real breakthrough came in 1972, when the first full-length movie was filmed in Kuwait. Entitled *Bas Ya Bahr*, or *A Cruel Sea*, it tells the story of a boy who worked as a pearl

Filming War

One of Kuwait's foremost filmmakers, Walid al-Awadi, is well respected for his documentaries. His first film, *A Moment in Time*, recounts the Iraqi occupation of Kuwait in 1990 and 1991. During the invasion, al-Awadi worked with the underground resistance movement, secretly fighting against the Iraqis while also filming. The movie was released in 1995 and won awards at several international film festivals. Two years later, al-Awadi's second documentary came out. *Silence of the Volcanoes* tells the stories of Kuwaiti prisoners of war held in Iraq.

Al-Awadi—who splits his time between Kuwait, London, New York, and Los Angeles—filmed *Dreams without Sleep* in 2001. It documents the lives of people affected by the September 11, 2001, terrorist attacks on the World Trade Center in New York City. Al-Awadi happened to be in New York on the day of the attacks, and he had his video camera with him. He filmed reactions on the streets of New York that day. He continued to film some people as they came to grips with the changes in their lives brought on by the attacks. Al-Awadi has said that, in many ways, the experiences of New Yorkers reminded him of the difficulties faced by Kuwaitis during the Iraqi invasion. As an Arab and a

Muslim, he wanted to make a statement about "hope and peace and bringing different cultures together."

Al-Awadi went on to make a documentary about the Iraq War that began in 2003. Like his other films, it shows the impact of war and destruction rippling through the lives of ordinary people.

diver to earn the approval of his girlfriend's family. His father had been a pearl diver himself and had been severely injured in a shark attack. He wanted a better future for his son. The dramatic tale was directed by Khalid al-Saddiq. Many young Kuwaitis have followed in al-Saddiq's footsteps, pursuing careers in film, television, and other media.

Music

Kuwait's music scene includes everything from Bedouin tunes played on traditional instruments to modern music using the latest high-tech equipment. The Bedouin songs are played using instruments such as the *rababa*, a one-stringed violin; the *tabla*, a drum made from animal skins; the *oud*, the original

The rababa dates back to at least the eighth century. It may be the ancestor of the violin.

lute; and the *daff*, which is like a tambourine. These instruments are still used today, especially at traditional ceremonies and celebrations.

Sometimes singing accompanies Bedouin music. Traditional songs are usually sung by women. In the past, women would only sing for small, private gatherings, accompanied by little more than clapping, but today some female groups sing in public, performing special songs for weddings.

In the 1970s, a bluesy style of music called *sawt* became popular in Kuwait. The country's sawt musicians are popular throughout the Gulf region. The al-Budur Band has performed together for decades.

Nawal is one of Kuwait's pioneering female singers. She has been making records since 1983.

Marriage Traditions in Kuwait

When it comes to weddings, young Kuwaitis today are no longer bound by the traditions of the past. Many choose to begin their marriage much as Westerners do, with a ring and a white dress. But others follow a traditional Kuwaiti path to marriage.

Traditionally, both sets of parents must approve of the union. Parents often choose a partner for their child. The couple becomes officially engaged by registering in an Islamic court. This grants them the right to begin dating.

The groom's family makes a payment to the bride's family. This money is supposed to help provide for the bride if her husband dies or divorces her.

The actual wedding takes place at an Islamic court. Afterward, there are great feasts, which men and women usually enjoy separately. The women gather in a tent, where they can take off their veils. There, they sing, dance, and eat together. The bride wears her finest clothes. She often has her hands and feet adorned with temporary tattoos from a reddish-brown dye called henna.

The men, in their own tent, feast, dance, and smoke together. In some traditional settings, they slaughter a sheep. Eventually, the groom will enter the bride's tent, sit with her for a short time, and then the two leave together to begin their married life.

Soccer is the most popular sport in Kuwait. The Kuwait national team has had rising success in recent years, beating traditionally powerful teams like China.

Sports

Modern sports in Kuwait began in 1932, when the nation's first soccer team was formed. Today, soccer is played by young people across the country. Kuwait also has a national soccer team that plays in international competitions.

At one time, cross-country car rallies were a major sport in Kuwait. These events stopped after the Iraqi invasion of Kuwait. The unexploded land mines buried throughout the countryside posed too great a danger. In recent years, many of those mines have been located and removed, so car rallies are making a comeback.

Cricket is a bat and ball sport that developed in England. British oil company workers brought the game to Kuwait in the 1930s.

Kuwait in the Olympics

Kuwait first sent athletes to the Olympics in 1968, to run the marathon at the Summer Games in Mexico City. In 1972, Kuwaitis competed in track and field and swimming. Kuwaitis have participated in every Summer Olympics since then, in sports such as weight lifting, rowing, boxing, swimming, and diving. In the 2000 Summer Olympics in Sydney, Australia, Fahd al-Dihani (far right) became the first Kuwaiti to earn a medal. He won the bronze medal in the trapshooting competition.

Many Kuwaitis take part in sports such as archery, bowling, and ice-skating. There are also several basketball clubs. Water sports are popular as well. Kuwaitis enjoy speedboating, water-

Jet skiers zip around a pier in Kuwait City. Jet skiing is so popular in Kuwait that it sometimes draws complaints from swimmers who want to enjoy the water in peace.

skiing, yachting, and scuba diving. The clear waters near the coast, combined with abundant sealife, make diving enjoyable. Fishing is fun, too. Kuwaitis catch several small types of shark, barracuda, tuna, and mackerel off the coast, along with snapper, catfish, flounder, sole, and puffer fish.

Some people use long casting rods to try to catch fish off Kuwait's shores. Others use simple poles.

Daily Life
in Kuwait

Many factors influence the way Kuwaitis live their lives each day. Islam, family, Arab tradition, oil wealth, and modernization all join to create the Kuwaiti lifestyle. The country has changed greatly in the last two decades, and its residents both honor the past and embrace the present.

Opposite: **Traditional and modern are often side by side in Kuwait.**

Some Kuwaiti men enjoy spending time at traditional coffee shops, where they smoke water pipes called *narghiles.*

The staple of all Kuwaiti meals is rice. There are several ways to prepare it. Perhaps the most common dish in Kuwait is *mahbus*. In this dish, rice seasoned with saffron is topped with chicken or lamb mixed with vegetables and spices, and then covered with a tomato-paste sauce. Mahbus has many variations, so it can be enjoyed often without becoming boring. This dish was influenced by Kuwait's Bedouin past, when it was easiest to cook everything together in one pot.

Skewered grilled meat, called *shish kebab*, is also common in Kuwait. Typically, the meat is lamb, though beef is becoming more common. Kuwaitis do not eat pork, as Islam forbids it.

Shish kebab is a popular dish in Kuwait.

Maraj, another popular dish, is similar to mahbus, but in maraj the meat and vegetables are boiled or fried separately first. They are then mixed together with seasonings. Immigrants from Persia brought this dish with them.

Seafood is plentiful in Kuwait, and Kuwaitis typically enjoy it several times a week. Shrimp, crab, lobster, grouper, and red snapper are some favorites. Kuwaitis enjoy a variety of vegetables, too, including salads made with lettuce, radishes, cucumbers, tomatoes, and onion.

Seafood is popular in Kuwait. Each Kuwaiti eats an average of 27 pounds (12 kg) of seafood per year.

Sponge Cake

Sponge cake is a popular dessert in Kuwait. It is often served with a pomegranate sauce to add flavor and color.

2 eggs
$\frac{3}{4}$ cup confectioners' sugar
$\frac{3}{4}$ cup flour
$\frac{1}{2}$ tsp. baking powder
$\frac{1}{2}$ tsp. cardamom
A pinch of saffron
1 tsp. sesame seeds

In a mixing bowl, beat the eggs well and gradually beat in the sugar. Sift the flour and baking powder together. Combine the flour mixture with the egg mixture. Add the cardamom and saffron. Pour the batter into a greased 8-inch baking pan. Sprinkle sesame seeds on top. Bake at 350 degrees for 20 minutes.

Kuwaitis always offer tea or coffee to guests in their home. The tea is often flavored with spices such as cardamom or saffron.

Coffee and tea are the most popular drinks in Kuwait. They are served at meals, and hosts will offer them to all visitors throughout the day. It is considered impolite to refuse a cup of coffee or tea. Many people also drink mineral water, juice, and soft drinks. Drinking alcohol is illegal in Kuwait.

Kuwaitis often share meals at large family gatherings. This is an important part of their social life. Dining out at restaurants has become increasingly popular, however, and Kuwaitis can choose from many good restaurants that reflect the diversity of the immigrants who live there. A growing number of international chain restaurants, including Starbucks, Pizza Hut, and McDonald's, also serve residents. Traditional Arab coffee shops, called *maqhas*, are found in Kuwait as well.

The first McDonald's in Kuwait opened in 1994. By 2006, thirty-four McDonald's resturaunts were sprinkled across the country.

Clothing seen on the streets of Kuwait ranges from traditional Arab garb to casual styles worn throughout the Western world to the latest in high fashion. Men and women in Kuwait are free to choose what style of clothes to wear.

Men who choose traditional clothing wear a *dishdasha* or *thawb*, a long-sleeved garment that flows to the ground and is worn with light pants underneath. Dishdashas are made of light cotton for the warm summer months and dark wool in the winter. The dishdasha is worn with the traditional three-piece headgear. The first part is the *kaffiya*, a close-fitting cap. It's covered with the *gutra*, a square piece of cloth that

Most Kuwaiti men wear traditional clothing. The light, loose clothing helps them stay cool in the hot sun.

Many women in Kuwait wear Western clothes. When they go out in public, however, many cover their Western clothes with a traditional robe.

is folded in a triangle and placed on the head, with the ends hanging down over the shoulders. Light-colored gutras are worn in the summer. They are replaced by red-checked gutras in cooler weather. Topping it off is the *agal*, a circle of black cord that holds it all in place.

Women in Kuwait who choose traditional clothing typically wear an *abayya*, a full-length silky black robe. Some may also wear a *burqa*, a dark veil that covers the face. Another choice is the *dara'a*, a loose-fitting long dress, often of beautiful colors. Other women wear the *hijab*, a scarf that covers the hair while exposing the face, but this is not traditional Kuwaiti fashion, and those wearing it usually come from other Muslim countries.

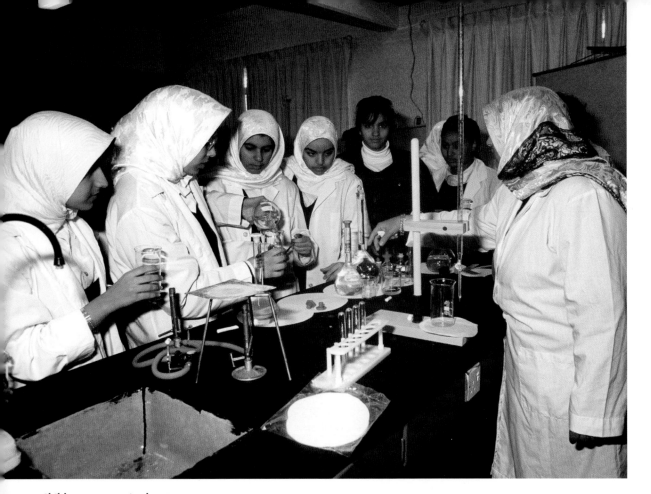

Children are required to attend school from ages six through fourteen. Seventy-nine percent of girls and 75 percent of boys go on to secondary school.

Health and Education

Kuwait is a wealthy nation, and the government makes sure its citizens have high-quality education and health care.

Kuwait began to invest heavily in its schools in the early 1950s, shortly after the oil money started flowing in. Today, its education system is considered among the best in the Middle East. All citizens get a free education, beginning with preschool for children ages four through six. Elementary, intermediate, and secondary schools each last four years. The government also provides a free college education to its citizens at Kuwait University. It will even pay for students to attend universities outside the country. More than fifteen thousand students attend Kuwait University each year, and some two thousand study abroad.

The government also provides classes for adults who did not learn to read as children. Because of this effort and the high-quality education for children, 84 percent of Kuwaitis can read. This is one of the highest literacy rates in the Middle East.

Health care in Kuwait improved greatly following the discovery of oil and is also free for all citizens. Kuwaitis can expect to live seventy-seven years, longer than in any other Middle Eastern nation. Few countries in the world offer such good health benefits as Kuwait. And oil money pays for it all.

Eighty-one percent of adult women can read. Here, women attend a class in which they study the Qur'an.

Time to Relax

The Gulf coast is the best place in Kuwait to cool off on a hot day. Kuwait City has made the most of this, building a large waterfront complex. It includes five public beaches, swimming pools, and an ice-skating rink. A large marina has room for hundreds of yachts. Just offshore is Green Island which the Kuwaitis built. Visitors can reach the island by a walkway. There, they can stroll through beautiful gardens, enjoy children's areas, relax in restaurants, and take in a show.

The Kuwait Towers loom over the coastline in Kuwait City. The tallest of the three reaches a height of 614 feet (187 m).

Kuwait's National Holidays

New Year's Day	January 1
National Day	February 25
Liberation Day	February 26

The following holidays are based on the Islamic calendar. Their dates change from year to year in the calendar used in the West.

'Id al-Fitr	A three-day celebration at the end of Ramadan
'Id al-Adha	A three-day holiday following the pilgrimage to Mecca
Islamic New Year	The first day of Muharram
Mawlid al-Nabi (Muhammad's birthday)	During the month of Rabi' al-Awwal
Al-Isra w'al-Mi'raj	The twenty-seventh day of the month of Rajab

Kuwaitis also like to pass the time shopping. The country has many modern malls and stores. But sometimes, Kuwaitis prefer the more traditional experience of shopping at *suqs*. These are open markets with many small shops. In Kuwait City, the covered suq is in the center of the city. It has about twenty different markets attached, each specializing in a certain type of item. Other Kuwaiti cities have suqs as well. Meats, fruits, vegetables, and bakery items are all sold in suqs.

The Hunter

Children in Kuwait and throughout the Gulf region enjoy playing a traditional game called the hunter. It's played with a group of about five to ten children. One child is selected to be the hunter. This child closes his or her eyes while the others scatter to find hiding places. Then the hunter has to try to find all the players and tag them while they try to run away. A hunter who doesn't catch all the others becomes the hunter again. If all the other children do get caught, then the first one to be tagged becomes the hunter.

A Kuwaiti Invention

Kuwait's many speedy drivers may have helped inspire an invention. Kuwait's Ahmad al-Hashash has created protective clothing to wear while riding motorcycles. He devised a way to put airbags into shirts, jackets, and suits. The airbags inflate to protect the rider in case of an accident.

Al-Hashash displayed his invention at the 2005 International Exhibition of Inventions in Geneva, Switzerland. He was awarded the Inventor's Oscar prize for his entry. Visitors chose it as their favorite from among the more than one thousand inventions from forty-two countries.

The markets also offer beautiful fabrics and clothing, furniture, jewelry and gold, and even electronics. Customers bargain for the best price, and shoppers can usually find some good deals.

Driving is a social activity in Kuwait, especially among young people. Nice cars are a status symbol. But there is growing concern among Kuwaitis that too many young people drive too fast and too aggressively. To combat this, police are enforcing speed and seat-belt laws more strictly. More drivers' education programs are also being offered to teach young drivers the importance of safe habits.

Kuwaiti drivers are famously reckless. They have a reputation for driving very fast and weaving in and out of traffic.

Desert Camping

Many Kuwaiti families enjoy camping together in the desert. The camping season begins in the spring, when visitors line the highways through the desert with white tents. People drive all-terrain vehicles and carry cell phones and handheld video games. They bring generators to power televisions, heaters, and air conditioners. They carry plenty of food and water—some even bring cooks and maids with them. It's not much like the real Bedouin experience, but it does give Kuwaitis an enjoyable taste of their history. And the entire family is together enjoying the pleasant spring weather. Many Kuwaiti children look forward to their camping trip each year.

Desert camping is one of the ways Kuwaitis blend the past and present. Kuwaitis face new challenges as they move into the future. But no matter what happens, they will continue to draw strength from their long, proud traditions.

Kuwaiti tents are not like Western camping tents. Instead, they're like Bedouin tents, which are shaped more like small circus tents.

Timeline

Kuwaiti History

Mubarak murders his brother, Shaikh Muhammad, and takes control of Kuwait.	1896
Shaikh Mubarak signs a treaty with the British to protect Kuwait.	1899
Kuwait's eastern border is defined.	1913
The Kuwait Oil Company begins exploratory drilling.	1936
Oil is discovered.	1938
Oil drilling is halted during World War II.	1939–1945
Kuwait and the Kuwait Oil Company sign an agreement granting Kuwait half of the oil production profits.	1951
Kuwait gains full independence; Iraq threatens to invade.	1961
The Kuwaiti constitution is approved.	1962
Kuwait's border with Saudi Arabia is agreed upon.	1966
Kuwait takes part in an oil embargo during the Arab-Israeli War.	1973
Shaikh Jabir al-Ahmad al-Sabah becomes amir.	1977
Iran bombs Kuwaiti oil wells.	1981
Iraq invades Kuwait.	1990
Coalition forces drive Iraq out of Kuwait.	1991
Shaikh Jabir al-Ahmad al-Sabah dies.	2006

World History

1914	World War I breaks out.
1917	The Bolshevik Revolution brings communism to Russia.
1929	A worldwide economic depression begins.
1939	World War II begins.
1945	World War II ends.
1957	The Vietnam War starts.
1969	Humans land on the Moon.
1975	The Vietnam War ends.
1989	The Berlin Wall is torn down as communism crumbles in Eastern Europe.
1991	The Soviet Union breaks into separate states.
2001	Terrorists attack the World Trade Center, New York, and the Pentagon, Washington, D.C.

Fast Facts

Official name: Dawlat al-Kuwayt (State of Kuwait)

Capital: Kuwait City

Official language: Arabic

Kuwait City

Kuwait's flag

Official religion: Islam

Year of founding: 1961

National anthem: "Al-Nashid al-Watani"

Government: Amirate

Chief of state: Amir

Head of government: Prime minister

Area: 6,880 square miles (17,818 km)

Greatest distance north to south 115 miles (185 km)

Greatest distance east to west 129 miles (208 km)

Land and water borders: Saudi Arabia to the south, Iraq to the north and west, the Persian Gulf to the east

Highest elevation: An unnamed hill, 1,004 feet (306 m) above sea level

Lowest elevation: Sea level, along the coastline

Average daily temperature: 91°F (33°C)

Average annual precipitation: 4 inches (10 cm)

National population (2006 est.): 2,418,393

Camel

Mosque in Salimiya

Currency

Population of largest cities (2005):

Qalib al-Shuyukh	179,264
Salimiya	145,328
Hawalli	106,992
Janub Khitan	92,646
al-Farwaniyah	83,544

Famous landmarks:
- ▶ *Kuwait Towers,* Kuwait City
- ▶ *Tariq Rajab Museum,* Hawalli
- ▶ *National Museum,* Kuwait City
- ▶ *The covered suq,* Kuwait City
- ▶ *The Grand Mosque,* Kuwait City
- ▶ *National Assembly Building*, Kuwait City

Industry: Oil dominates Kuwait's economy. It accounts for the vast majority of its income and 90 percent of its exports. A small amount of manufacturing takes place in Kuwait. The products made include fertilizer, cement, and bricks. Only 1 percent of Kuwait is farmland. The major agriculture products grown include chickens, milk, tomatoes, and potatoes.

Currency: The Kuwaiti dinar. In 2006, .29 dinar equaled 1 U.S. dollar

System of weights and measures: Metric system

Literacy (2003 est.): 84 percent

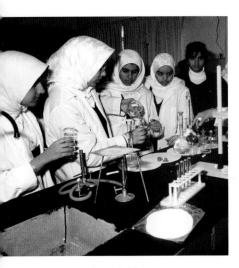
Schoolchildren

Shaikh Jabir al-Ahmad al-Sabah

Common Arabic words and phrases:

Insha'allah	God willing
Salâm alaykum	Peace be with you
Shukran	Thank you
Asif	I am sorry
Wáalid	Father
Wáalidah	Mother
Akh	Brother
Ukht	Sister
Jáahil	Child

Famous Kuwaitis:

Shaikh Sabah bin Jabir (c. late 1600s–1762)
First amir of Kuwait

Mubarak the Great (1837–1915)
Amir of Kuwait, 1896–1915

Shaikh al-Sabah al-Ahmad al-Sabah (1928–)
Current amir of Kuwait

Shaikh Jabir al-Ahmad al-Sabah (1928–2006)
Amir of Kuwait, 1977–2006

Mas'uma al-Mubarak (1951–)
First woman cabinet minister

Walid al-Awadi (1969–)
Filmmaker

To Find Out More

Books

▶ Korman, Susan. *Kuwait*. Philadelphia: Chelsea House Publishers, 2003.

▶ Miller, Debra A. *Kuwait*. Detroit: Thomson Gale, 2005.

▶ Ray, Kurt. *A Historical Atlas of Kuwait*. New York: Rosen Publishing Group, 2004.

▶ Santella, Andrew. *The Persian Gulf War*. Minneapolis: Compass Point Books, 2004.

Web Sites

▶ **Kuwait Cultural Profiles Project**
www.cp-pc.ca/english/kuwait/index.html
For information on Kuwait's geography, family life, sports, food, education, holidays, and more.

▶ **Kuwait Information Office**
www.kuwait-info.com
For current news and cultural information about Kuwait.

▶ **One World—Nations Online: Kuwait**
www.nationsonline.org/oneworld/
kuwait.htm
To find basic facts about Kuwait and a wide variety of links.

Organizations and Embassies

▶ **Kuwaiti Embassy in Canada**
80 Elgin Street
Ottawa, ON K1P 1C6
613-780-9999

▶ **Kuwaiti Embassy in the United States**
2940 Tilden Street NW
Washington, DC 20008
202-966-0702

Index

Page numbers in *italics* indicate illustrations.

Gulf Oil Corporation, 46
Gulf War, 11–12, *12*, 19, *20*, 22–23, *52*, *53*, 54–55, 56, 69, *75*, 105
gutra (clothing), 120–121

H
hajj (fifth pillar of Islam), 96, 99
al-Hashash, Ahmad, 126
Hawalli, 25, 54, 77
health care, 47, 82, 123
henna, 109
hijab (clothing), 121
Hijra ("Migration"), 91
Hijri calendar. *See* Islamic calendar.
Hinduism, 90
historical maps. *See also* maps.
 Early Regional History, *37*
 Gulf War (1990–1991), *52*
 Neutral Zone (1922–1969), *48*
holidays
 national, 125
 religious, 92, 95–96, 98–99
horses, 32, *32*
House of Islamic Antiquities, 105
hunter (game), 125
Hussein, Saddam, 11, 51, *51*, *53*, 54, 55

I
'Id al-Adha (feast), 98, 99, *99*, 125
'Id al-Fitr (feast), 98–99, 125
Ikaros colony, 38
Indus River valley, 37
insect life, 33, 34
International Exhibition of Inventions (Geneva), 126
Inventor's Oscar prizes, 126
Iran-Iraq War, 50–51
Iraq, 11, 12, 16, 17, *18*, 23, 37, 43, 45, 47, 49, 51, 52, 53, 55, 57, 105, 106

Islamic calendar, 92, 95, 125
Islamic Jihad militant group, 49
Islamic New Year, 125
Islamic religion, 43, 63, 65, 67, 88, 89, 91–92, *92*, 93, 94–95, 97, 98, 101, 102, 109, 115, 116. *See also* religion.

J
Jabir, Shaikh Sabah ibn, 42
al-Jalahimah, Rahmah bin Jabir, *43*
Janub Khitan, 25, 77
jerboas, 33
Judaism, 93
judicial branch of government, 61, 62–63, *63*
Justice Palace, 63

K
Ka'ba shrine, 96
kaffiya (clothing), 120
al-Khalifa family, 41
Kinda Empire, 38
Kuwait Airways, 50
Kuwait Bay, 22, 25, 40
Kuwait City, 9, *21*, 22, 25, 37, 46, 49, 52, 58, *59*, 66–67, *66*, *67*, 75, 79, 89, *94*, 105, 124, *124*
Kuwait Oil Company, 46, 47
Kuwait Towers, *67*, *124*
Kuwait University, 62, 122, 123

L
land mines, 22, 53, 111
landscape, 17, 23
languages
 Arabic, 84–85, *84*
 body language, 87, *87*
 calligraphy, 85

Meet the Author

WHEN SHE ISN'T WRITING BOOKS FOR YOUNG PEOPLE, Terri Willis can often be found in the classroom, working directly with students as a substitute teacher. She enjoys the opportunity to spend time in elementary and middle schools. "I really like substitute teaching," she says. "There's so much variety in it! I often don't know what I'll be called on to do on any given day. Some people wouldn't like that, but to me, it makes it interesting."

The work, she feels, is a good complement to her work as an author. She's often required to teach a topic on short notice. While she's familiar with most subjects that the students are discussing, she needs to figure out quickly how to communicate the material in a way that makes sense. "That's a lot of what I do as an author, too," Terri says. "I read and research and study all types of materials. Some of it is highly technical and would be difficult for young people to understand. It is my job to take that information, figure out what is important to include in the book, and present it clearly.

"Working directly with students gives me an insight into how to approach topics with them. In fact, sometimes when I'm stuck while writing, I'll imagine that I'm trying to explain the material to a specific student I've taught recently, and go from there."

Terri's work on Kuwait began at her local library, where she checked out all the books she could find on the country. Several days of reading give her a good base of knowledge. Then it was time to start filling in details, the interesting tidbits that add so much understanding. Universities, embassies, and the Internet were all good sources.

"I got really excited when I read about the robots shaped like little boys that they are now using for camel races in Kuwait," Terri says. "It's such a good illustration of the connection there between ancient tradition and modern technology."

Terri has written several other books about the Middle East for the Enchantment of the World series, including *Lebanon*, *Qatar*, and *Libya*. She also wrote *Romania*, *Vietnam*, *Venezuela*, and *Democratic Republic of the Congo* for the series.

Terri has a degree in journalism from the University of Wisconsin-Madison. She lives in Cedarburg, Wisconsin, with her husband, Harold, and their daughters, Andrea and Liza.

Photo Credits

Photographs © 2007:

age fotostock/Alberto Ramella/Marka: 121
Alamy Images: 75 (Adrian Arbib), 7 top, 25 top, 117 (Keith Erskine), 33 (Juniors Bildarchiv), 30 (Papilio), 118 (Penny Tweedie)
Animals Animals/McKinnon Films/OSF/ Earth Scenes: 53
AP/Wide World Photos/Gustavo Ferrari: 10, 64, 83, 86
Art Directors and TRIP Photo Library: 103, 104 (Juliet Highet), 15, 36, 71, 73, 89, 93, 113, 122, 123, 132 bottom, 133 top (Helene Rogers), 28
Corbis Images: 40 (Archivo Iconografico, S.A.), 20, 63 top, 69, 127 (Yann Arthus-Bertrand), 31, 41 (Bettmann), 49, 133 bottom (Patrick Durand/Sygma), 112 top (Haslin/Sygma), 45 (E. O. Hoppé), 29 (Hanan Isachar), 27 (Steve Kaufman), 60 (Kuwaiti Information Ministry/epa), 56 (Damir Sagolj/Reuters), 46 (Peter Skingley/Bettmann), 12, 74 (Peter Turnley), 38 (Sandro Vannini)
Getty Images: 81, 82 (Essam Al-Sudani/ AFP), 24, 62, 79, 94, 95, 110, 114, 115, 120 (Yasser Al-Zayyat/AFP), 2 (Mark Daffey/Lonley Planet Images), 112 bottom (Richard Ellis), 109 (Tim Graham), 106 (Scott Gries), 32, 108 (Karim Jaafar/AFP), 51 (Mike Nelson/AFP), 126 (Gary John Norman/Stone), 98, 99, 119 (Joe Raedle), 59, 66, 130 (Pankaj & Insy Shah/Gulfimages)

Images & Stories/Izzet Keribar: 58, 80, 84, 124
JupiterImages/Eric Futran/FoodPix: 116
Lonely Planet Images: cover, 6, 9, 17, 21, 22, 61, 76, 78, 87, 90, 100, 111, (Mark Daffey), 101 (Christine Osborne)
MapQuest.com, Inc.: 63 bottom, 131 top
Mary Evans Picture Library: 92
Nature Picture Library Ltd.: 35 (Georgette Douwma), 34 (David Shale)
North Wind Picture Archives: 43, 44
Panos Pictures/Penny Tweedie: 77
Peter Arnold Inc./S. Compoint/UNEP: 55
Photo Researchers, NY/David Parker: 26, 131 bottom
photolibrary.com/JTB Photo Communications Inc: 7 bottom, 97, 107
Superstock, Inc./age fotostock: 85
The Image Works: 70 (Alex Farnsworth), 25 bottom, 132 top (Markus Heimbach/ Visum), 42 (Mary Evans Picture Library), 16 (Topham), 8, 14, 18, 39, 68, 88 (Charles Walker/Topfoto), 102, 105 (Charles Walker/Topham)

Maps and Illustrations by XNR Productions, Inc.